# THE KING JAMES BIBLE'S ACCURACY & FAITHFULNESS

## *A CELEBRATION*

## (Historical Quotes About The KJB)

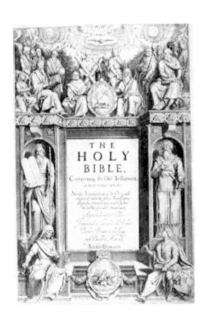

### H. D. Williams, M.D., Ph.D.

KJB RESEARCH COUNCIL

> **Disclaimer**
>
> The author of this work has quoted the writers of many articles and books. This does not mean that the author endorses or recommends the works of others. If the author quotes someone, it does not mean that he agrees with all of the author's tenets, statements, concepts, or words, whether in the work quoted or any other work of the author. There has been no attempt to alter the meaning of the quotes; and therefore, some of the quotes are long in order to give the entire sense of the passage.

Copyright © 2011 by H. D. Williams
All Rights Reserved
Printed in the United States of America
REL067030: Religion: Christian Theology - Apologetics

**ISBN: 978-0-9846553-0-4**

All Scripture quotes are from the King James Bible except those verses compared and then the source is identified.

No part of this work may be reproduced without the expressed consent of the publisher, except for brief quotes, whether by electronic, photocopying, recording, or information storage and retrieval systems.

Address All Inquiries To:
THE OLD PATHS PUBLICATIONS, INC.
142 Gold Flume Way
Cleveland, Georgia, 30528
U.S.A.

Web: www.theoldpathspublications.com
E-mail: TOP@theoldpathspublications.com

1.0

KJB RESEARCH COUNCIL

# DEDICATION

This work is dedicated to my 5 great-grandchildren, Owen, Matthew, Emmaline, Leah, and Graham. In the years to come, may God guide each of them to His Truth in the English language, the King James Bible.

# THE KJB'S ACCURACY & FAITHFULNESS

Infinite is the debt of gratitude which the world owes to its Maker for the Bible. Scarcely less is its debt to his goodness in raising up competent instruments for its translation into different tongues, unlocking its treasures to enrich the nations. (Andrew McClure, *The Translators Revived*, 1855, pp. 223-224, pp. 230-231 in the PDF)

# TABLE OF CONTENTS

DEDICATION ..................................................................... 3
TABLE OF CONTENTS ..................................................... 5
ABREVIATIONS ................................................................ 9
PREFACE ........................................................................ 11
INTRODUCTION ............................................................. 13
    The Reasons for This Work ................................. 13
    What is Accuracy and Faithfulness? .................... 16
    Faithfulness ......................................................... 18
    The Purpose of This Work ................................... 19
    Critics of the AV/KJB .......................................... 20
    An Example: Dr. Richard Kilby's Experience .......... 21
    Not This Author's Words ..................................... 22
    The Organization of the Work ............................. 23
    Importance of Vernacular Translations ................ 24
    The Difficulties of Translating ............................. 26
    Quotes of Sciolists Opposed to the AV/KJB .......... 27
    Examples of Sciolists .......................................... 30
    John Bellamy ...................................................... 30
    A FALSE CLAIM ................................................... 32
    Hugh Broughton .................................................. 36
**CHAPTER 1: QUOTES SUPPORTING THE AV/KJB TRANSLATION 1600s ................................................... 41**
    Richard Field, D.D. ............................................. 41
    Mr. Matthew Poole .............................................. 44
    John Selden ........................................................ 46
    Brian Walton ....................................................... 46
    Ludwig Cappellus ................................................ 47
    AV/KJB Translators ............................................. 49
    The Translators Identified .................................. 49
**CHAPTER 2: QUOTES SUPPORTING THE AV/KJB TRANSLATION 1700s ................................................... 51**
    Jonathan Swift ................................................... 51
    Alexander Geddes ............................................... 52
    Samuel Horsley .................................................. 53
    Dr. Robert Gray .................................................. 54
    Robert Lowth ...................................................... 55

# THE KJB'S ACCURACY & FAITHFULNESS

**CHAPTER 3: QUOTES SUPPORTING THE AV/KJB TRANSLATION 1800s .................................................. 57**
    Quarterly Review .................................................. 57
    Thomas Rennell, D.D. .......................................... 58
    Thomas Fanshawe Middleton ............................. 61
    Dr. Adam Clarke .................................................. 61
    Dean John William Burgon ................................. 63
    Solomon Caesar Malan ....................................... 67
    Alexander Wilson McClure ................................. 76

**CONCLUSION .................................................................. 83**
    Dr. D. A. Waite's Conclusion .............................. 85

**APPENDIX ...................................................................... 89**
    THE TRANSLATORS ............................................. 89
    1. Lancelot Andrewes. ........................................ 90
    2. John Overal. .................................................... 90
    3. Adrian Saravia. ............................................... 90
    4. Dr. Richard Clarke. ......................................... 90
    5. Dr. Layfield. .................................................... 91
    6. Dr. Teigh. ........................................................ 91
    7. Mr. Burgley, or Burleigh. ................................ 91
    8. Mr. (h) Geoffry King. ...................................... 92
    9. Mr. Thomson. .................................................. 92
    10. William Bedwell. .......................................... 92
    11. Edward Lively. .............................................. 93
    XII. John Richardson. .......................................... 95
    XIII. Laurence Chaderton. .................................. 95
    XIV. Francis Dillingham. ..................................... 96
    XV. Thomas Harrison. ........................................ 96
    XVI. Roger Andrewes ......................................... 96
    XVII. Robert Spalding. ........................................ 96
    XVIII Andrew Byng. ........................................... 97
    XIX. Dr. John Harding. ....................................... 97
    XX. Dr. John Rainolds, or Reinolds. .................. 97
    XXI. Thomas Holland. ........................................ 97
    XXII. Rickard Kilby ............................................. 98
    XXIII. Miles Smith. .............................................. 99
    XXIV. Dr. Richard Brett. ..................................... 99
    XXV. Mr. Fairclough, or Fairclowe. .................. 100
    XXVI. William Barlow. ...................................... 100
    XXVII. Dr. Hutchinson, or Hutckeson. .............. 100
    XXVIII. Dr. Spencer. .......................................... 100

XXIX. Mr. Fenton. ............................................... 101
XXX. Mr. Rabbell. ............................................. 101
XXXI. Mr. Sanderson. ......................................... 101
XXXII. William Dakins. ....................................... 101
XXXIII. Thomas Ravis. ........................................ 101
XXXIV. George Abbot. ........................................ 102
XXXV. Rickard Eedes. ......................................... 102
XXXVI. Giles Tomson. ........................................ 103
XXXVII. Mr. Savile. ............................................ 103
XXXVIII. John Perin. .......................................... 103
XXXIX. Dr. Ravens. ............................................ 103
XL. John Harmar. .............................................. 103
XLI. John Duport, D.D. ....................................... 104
XLII. Dr. William Branthwait. ................................ 104
XLIII. Jeremiah Radcliffe. .................................... 104
XLIV. Samuel Ward. .......................................... 104
XLV. Andrew Downes. ........................................ 105
XLVI. John Bois. .............................................. 105
XLVII. Mr. Ward. .............................................. 106
Archbishop Bancroft .......................................... 106
Thomas Bilson ................................................ 107
**INDEX** ............................................................ **113**
**ABOUT THE AUTHOR** ....................................... **119**
BOOKS BY DR. WILLIAMS ................................ 120
THE MIRACLE OF BIBLICAL INSPIRATION ........... 120
WORD-FOR-WORD TRANSLATING OF THE RECEIVED TEXT, VERBAL PLENARY TRANSLATING: ............. 121
THE ATTACK ON THE CANON OF SCRIPTURE, A POLEMIC AGAINST MODERN SCHOLARSHIP ........ 121
THE LIE THAT CHANGED THE MODERN WORLD ... 122
THE PURE WORDS OF GOD ............................. 122
WYCLIFFE CONTROVERSIES ............................ 123
HEARING THE VOICE OF GOD ......................... 123
ORIGIN OF THE CRITICAL TEXT ....................... 123
THE COVENANT OF SALT ................................ 124

## Criticism of the RT & AV/KJB is Not New

In 1869, S. C. Malan said: "A man who, like him (the Dean of Canterbury), sets to a work of this kind, apparently without the slightest hesitation or misgiving in his own powers, thinking it the easiest thing in the world to make wholesale changes in the Greek text and in the joint labours of more than fifty learned men of old, instead of dealing with the utmost reverence and caution, not only forms an unworthy estimate of the work he undertakes- but he also recklessly wounds the feeling of deep respect and affection with which men, nowise his inferiors in judgment or scholarship, still continue to look upon the Received Text and the English Bible. Both these have, indeed, lasted more than two centuries; a long time, in truth, for those who think that wisdom, learning, and scholarship have only just dawned on the land, and that, until now, all was darkness and ignorance. Wise men, however, do not think so; but rather take the long life of those two monuments of ancient piety and learning as a proof of their real merit and excellence. And while such men readily give the Dean of Canterbury full credit for his plodding industry, and also for sundry useful hints in his renderings- they yet, on the whole, confess, that a better acquaintance with his work only tends **to deepen their reverence and to strengthen their affection for their old friends and companions, the Received Greek Text of the New Testament and the Authorised Version of it—neither of which they ever intend to give up; not even at the Dean's bidding."** (Rev. S. C. Malan, M.A., *A Plea for the Received Greek Text and for the Authorised Version of the New Testament in Answer to Some of the Dean of Canterbury's Criticisms on Both,* London, 1869, pp. 211-212) (my emphasis, HDW)

# ABREVIATIONS

| | |
|---|---|
| *a priori* | "prior to" based on something known, assumed or known without reference to experience. |
| AV | Authorized Version, spelled Authorised in England |
| B.D. | Bachelor of Divinity |
| c. | circa, about |
| D.D. | Doctor of Divinity, a graduate degree in England, and honorary degree in America. |
| e.g. | *exempli gratia*, means "for example," or "for instance" |
| en.wikipedia | English Wikipedia Encyclopedia |
| i.e. | *id est, means "that is"* |
| KJB | King James Bible, also called the King James Version |
| LXX | 70, refers to the Septuagint; allegedly and falsely attributed to 70 Jewish translators who translated the Old Testament in 70 days. |
| NA | Nestles Aland Text |
| p. | page |
| pp. | pages |
| q.v. | *quod videre* means "which to see" |
| RT | Received Text |
| TR | Textus Receptus, means the "Received Text" |
| USB | United Bible Society |
| v.s. | vide supra, means "see above" |
| viz. | videlicet, means "namely" |

"Nothing could be more right and proper than the making, in the reign of James I, that wonderful Translation of the Bible—**wonderful** both f**or purity of language and accuracy of interpretation.**" ("Liturgical Reform," *Quarterly Review*, Jan., 1834, p. 541; also in Todd's 3rd Edition) (my emphasis, HDW)

# PREFACE

Dr Williams has rendered a great service to all students of the King James Bible. His masterful historical research demonstrates that there have always been critics of the King James Bible but their criticisms are willful and not scholarly. Genuine scholars have repeatedly risen to its defense and promotion. They still do. This book is a great resource in the study of the history of the King James Bible. I recommend it to any serious student of the King James Bible.

>Phil Stringer, Ph.D.
>Senior Pastor
>Ravenswood Baptist Church
>4455 N. Seeley
>Chicago, IL 60625

Thank you Dr. Williams for your excellent, careful research in putting together this book, *The King James Bible's Accuracy & Faithfulness.* Consistently I receive correspondence from a self-appointed "scholar" who takes the King James Bible to task for some shortcoming and who lauds some new English translation of the Bible. What I find interesting is that I have a shelf full of "orphan" Bible versions that have been published, which claim that their new translation will replace the antiquated King James Bible. Yet, the King James Bible edures! It has endured for 400 years and will continue.

As you read this book, and digest the content, you will understand why the King James Bible has endured! God's hand was upon the translators! They were

KJB RESEARCH COUNCIL

# THE KJB'S ACCURACY & FAITHFULNESS

meticulous in their translation of the Hebrew, Aramaic and Greek texts they used. The precision in the choices for their words and phrases is unparalleled in ANY other English translation. You will understand why I say this when you read the quotes from men in the 1600s, 1700s and 1800s.

I believe reading this book will deepen your reverence and strengthen your affection for our King James Bible. There is no need for revising or correcting it! Indeed, abandoning the King James Bible, as many have done, is a grave error. They are exchanging gold for fool's gold.

> David L. Brown, Ph.D.
> Senior Pastor
> First Baptist Church
> 10550 S. Howell Avenue
> Oak Creek, WI  53154

# INTRODUCTION

## The Reasons for This Work

For a number of years, this author has noted a plethora of writers, both in the past and in recent days, who denigrate the accuracy and faithfulness of the King James Bible (KJB), which is known as the Authorized Version (AV) in England. Initially, the charges by the critics against the AV/KJB translation and the translators caused me significant concern. Were they right? Therefore, over the next few years, I endeavored to evaluate a number of their charges.

In reaction to the claims of the critics, the underlying Hebrew and Greek text of the AV/KJB was consulted many times. Although the author does not allege to be a linguistic scholar, the tools God has provided, such as lexicons, dictionaries and concordances, were used to compare the critics' assertions with the AV/KJB translator's rendering of the "received" Hebrew, Aramaic, and Greek texts. In almost every instance that was evaluated, what I noticed is the predilection for the critics to prefer THEIR words over the words of the KJB translators. There seemed to be no regard for polysemy (a word having multiple meanings), context, **and** signification by the 'self-exalting' critics. Signification is "the nuances or differences of the meaning of a word in a specific context."

As we shall see, Dr. Richard Kilby, one of the translators of the AV/KJB, reported that during the translation process they considered MANY words for a particular "original" word in Hebrew, Aramaic, and Greek in a passage, but consistently chose the one

# THE KJB'S ACCURACY & FAITHFULNESS

English word that had the closest signification or correlation to the context of the passage.

Unfortunately, there is little information in the literature concerning the exact translating methods of the Cambridge, Oxford, and Westminster Companies in 1611, which were split into six committees. It is believed a large number of documents were lost in the "Great Fire of London" in 1666. However, one of the most important translators, John Bois, left some notes that were found in 1964. A website made the following comment:

> These notes were lost from 1688 until 1964, when Professor Ward Allen located a handwritten copy among the papers of William Fulham, a seventeenth century antiquarian and collector, whose papers were in the Corpus Christi College Library at Oxford University. (http://the-holdfast.blogspot.com/)

The manuscript Ward Allen found and presented in his book, *Translating For King James, Notes Made by a Translator of King James's Bible,* is a treasure without a doubt. The work reflects the deepest considerations for selecting the proper English words by the translators. Allen said:

> John Bois, Andrew Downes, and their fellow translators are now my old companions. This acquaintance has made clear just what John Selden meant when he wrote that Andrew Downes was "most excellent" in Greek and just why Sir Henry Savile gave John Bois approbation [approval] for his notes on St. John Chrysostom's homilies. **The translators of the Authorized Version had great learning and subtle minds.**

## INTRODUCTION

(Allen, *Translating For King James,* Vanderbilt Press, 1969, p.v).

After this author read the qualifications of Bois, Downes, Selden, and Savile, the comment above came to life. For that reason and many others, the appendix contains information on the translators of the AV/KJB from several of the earliest compilations about them.

I am pleased to report that after years of consideration, I believe Dr. Allen to be absolutely correct. The critics' requests over the centuries for "revisions," or for "corrections" of the translating, or for even abandoning the AV/KJB were, and still are, very unjustified. Their claims are simply "plain wrong."

It is obvious to students of the Scripture that God had a providential hand in the translating of the King James Bible. The translation was made in *"the fullness of time,"* so to speak, because of the spirituality, learning, and scholarship present in England in the sixteen hundreds. Furthermore, God's *"right hand of power"* was evident in the translation. God knew that the work of the translators was going to have international influence, which continues to this day. This fact cannot be overstated.

Finally, the assertion can be made by this author that there are **no** translational errors in the AV/KJB! There are **no** "better" words. There are **no** better-trained men to translate. The product, the King James Bible, is absolutely a superior work of God and men that will never be repeated for English-speaking people.

## What is Accuracy and Faithfulness?

We must begin by defining accuracy and faithfulness. Technically speaking, <u>accuracy</u> refers to the <u>degree of conformity</u> of a measure to the actual, true value.

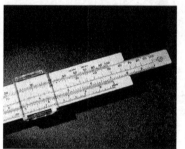

<u>Precision</u> is simply <u>the degree of refinement</u> with which a measure can be taken or stated. So, for example, 0.98597632 is a very precise number; 1.0 is much less precise.

A slide rule is never perfectly accurate; it is only representative of the true value. A slide rule is never perfectly precise; it is precise only to the third or fourth decimal place.

The "original" Words of God are *infinitely* and *eternally* **accurate** because they are *"given by inspiration of God."* They are *"pure words: as silver tried in a furnace of earth, purified seven times."* They are settled in Heaven *"for ever"* (Psa. 119:89; 12:6-7). Translations of His God-breathed Words should be as accurate and faithful to the "original" Words as man can achieve because they are the Words "breathed-out" by the One and Only Almighty Omnipotent, Omniscient, Omnipresent God, which were *"once delivered"* (Jude 3).

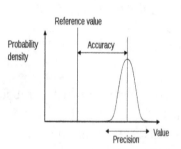

## INTRODUCTION

God "breathed-out" the Words that were to be recorded by the apostles and prophets. They simply wrote the "breathed-out" Words down (2 Pe. 1:21). Those Words are infinitely and eternally **precise**. The word "original" refers to the inerrant, infallible *"once delivered"* Words which are our *"foundation;"* that is, our *"faith"* (Jude 3, Ephesians 2:20). Our faith is composed of doctrines derived from the perfect Words from a perfect God (Deuteronomy 32:4, 2 Samuel 22:31, Psalm 18:30). The AV/KJB preserves the perfection, precision, and accuracy of those Words in English. There are **no** mistakes. There are **no** conflicts or disagreements within the sixty-six books of the Bible. This claim cannot be made by the modern versions.

As an example, Dr. J. A. Moorman has demonstrated that the modern versions cannot be used for Biblical chronology because the "numbers" in the texts are wrong; only the KJB is correct (Dr. Jack Moorman, *Bible Chronology, The Two Great Divides, A Defense of the Unbroken Biblical Chronology from Adam to Christ,* Bible For Today Press, 2010, p. 5).

We can call the AV/KJB translation "the Words of God in English." God has granted authority to His Words that are accurately and faithfully translated into English, or any language, because of His commands to *"Go ye therefore, and teach all nations . . ."* and *"Go ye into all the world, and preach the gospel to every creature"* (Matthew 28:19, Matthew 16:15). Unless nationals or language-groups have proper translations based upon the proper texts in Hebrew, Aramaic, and Greek, how can His commandments be obeyed; how can *"the gospel be preached to every creature"*?

## Faithfulness

The *faithfulness* of a translation refers to the **precision** and **accuracy** of the work. The closer the translator's words **reflect** the "original" Words, then the more accurate, or the better the "degree of **conformity**" to the "original" Words. The more **precise** or synonymous the words chosen by the translators are in context (called "signification"), then the closer the **refinement** of the translated text to the "original" Words in Hebrew, Aramaic, and Greek. The original Words were preserved for us as a foundation for translating (Psalm 12:6-7, Matthew 4:4, 24:35, etc., etc.). According to the best Biblical scholars, who are unsurpassable, the AV/KJB translation is superior in every way, as we shall see.

In another way, *faithfulness* engenders all the aspects of the doctrines of Biblical faith. Translators must trust and believe the God of the Bible. In order for men to be qualified translators, they must be men who are faithful to God, who are faithful to His Words, and who demonstrate obedience by their lives. The AV/KJB translators were faithful men. This author does not subscribe to the denigration of the translators by the secular book, *God's Secretaries,* written by Adam Nicholson. His work is entirely without references.

The King James Bible is a VERY accurate and faithful translation of the original. It is wonderfully accurate and precisely **faithful** to the Words that were breathed-out by God. Men and women hearing the Words in the King James Bible can be saved; that is, *"born again"* (John 3:7) Why? Because the Words in the AV/KJB are the Words of God in English and *"faith cometh by hearing*

## INTRODUCTION

*and hearing by the word of God"* (Romans 10:17). In other words, the AV/KJB is the Words of life in English. They will lead any man or woman who is willing to *"the fountain of living waters"* and thus, *"eternal life"* (Jeremiah 2:13, 17:13, John 6:68).

The 54 (some authors report 47) translators of the "Received Text" struggled at least from 1604 to 1610 to *choose* accurate and faithful words in English that were synonymous with the original Words and their "signification." Incidentally, the difference in the number of translators has to do with either those who died during the years dedicated to producing the translation, or to those not included in the original companies at Cambridge, Oxford, and Westminster, but were integrated later in the review process.

If the Words in the AV/KJB translation, which were chosen by the translators over 6 years were "breathed-out" by God, then the translation would have been completed in days. God does not need six, seven, or more years to complete a translation. Why did God require men to translate His Words instead of simply "breathing" them out? One obvious reason is that He wanted men in the church who would study His Words in depth and become intimately acquainted with them.

## The Purpose of This Work

The purpose of this work is not to belittle, castigate, or damage others. Neither is it to exalt anyone, particularly this author. Rather, the reasons are:

1. To encourage pastors, teachers, missionaries, evangelists, and 'the man in the pew' to believe (and know) that the AV/KJB translation is the

best English translation ever produced. It is the most accurate and faithful translation in English of the *"once delivered"* Words *"given"* to the Apostles and Prophets to record in Hebrew, Aramaic, and Greek as they were *"moved by the Holy Ghost"* (2 Tim. 3:16, 2 Pe. 1:19-21, Jude 3). The Words are those *"given by inspiration of God."* The process and product of inspiration was never to be repeated *"when that which is perfect is come"* (1 Cor. 13:10).

2. To praise and glorify the Lord Jesus Christ, our Saviour, who is called the Word of God (John 1:1, 14; 1 John 1:1). He has given to us the Words of life (John 6:68) for His glory and He alone is worthy (Rev. 4:11).

3. To honour the AV/KJB because of its accuracy and faithfulness to the "original" Words of God received in Hebrew, Aramaic, and Greek, which were preserved by God who worked through the nation Israel and the church to "keep them" (Psa. 12:6-7).

As the reader will discover, the words of unmatched, incredibly qualified defenders of the AV/KJB will echo the sentiments above.

## Critics of the AV/KJB

Often, those who criticize the AV/KJB translation are simply giving **their** preferred word(s) for translating the original Word(s). All too often, they make the grievous mistake of launching a venomous attack upon the translators and the AV/KJB text because they consider their words superior to those of the 54 or 47

# INTRODUCTION

translators. In other words, they are glorifying their words ALONE.

## An Example: Dr. Richard Kilby's Experience

A widely reported, good example of the tragedy of glorifying a person's words over the words chosen by the AV/KJB translation committees' words follows. It relates to one of the translators, Dr. Richard Kilby (also spelled Kilbie in the literature), who became the "rector" (religious administrator) of Lincoln College.

> Among the fruits of his learning, he left Commentaries on Exodus, chiefly formed from the monuments of the rabbins and Hebrew interpreters. Of the care and exactness, with which our translation was conducted, and which Dr. Kilby in his share had bestowed upon it, the following narrative by Isaac Walton, the most faithful of biographers, is a very gratifying evidence. Dr. Kilby and bishop Sanderson had, in early life, been intimate friends. The doctor was to ride a journey into Derbyshire, and took Mr. Sanderson to bear him company; and they resting on a Sunday with the doctor's friend, and going together to that parish church where they then were, found the young preacher to have no more discretion, that to waste a great part of the hour allotted for his sermon *in exception against the late translation* (the AV/KJB) *of several words,* (not expecting such a hearer as Dr. Kilbie,) and shewed three reasons why a particular word should have been otherwise translated. When Evening Prayer was ended, the preacher was invited to the doctor's friend's

> house, where after some other conference the doctor told him, he might have preached more useful doctrine, and not have filled his auditor's ears with *needless exceptions against the late Translation; and for that word, for which he offered to that poor congregation three reasons why it ought to have been translated as he said, he and others had considered all of them and found thirteen more considerable reasons why it was translated as now printed.* (Rev. Henry John Todd, M.A., Chaplain in Ordinary to his Majesty, and Archdeacon of Cleveland, *An Authentic Account of Our Authorized Translation of the Holy Bible, and of the Translators: With Testimonies to the Excellence of the Translation,* 2nd Edition, 1834, pp. 34-35)

Others criticize the translation because they accept the tenets of modern textual criticism, which has mutilated the underling text of the AV/KJB. In either case, this author has found that the disparagements are unfair criticism. This work will not examine the very technical details related to the Hebrew and Greek. Rather, quotes from authors who were linguists or scholars and unsurpassed in their abilities, will be presented.

## Not This Author's Words

The quotes throughout this work will be from several different centuries. They will be primarily from the works of Henry John Todd (1763 – 1845) and a few others. Todd was Chaplin in Ordinary to his Majesty, and Keeper of the Archbishop of Canterbury's records.

He states the reasons for writing his exposé for the "general reader" are the following:

# INTRODUCTION

1. "To teach him not to listen to any, who would chill his regard for it (the AV/KJB),

2. To furnish him with reasons, that there is no necessity for a new Translation,

3. To shew him that the Christian world has not hitherto sat in darkness, out of which it is now to be led by the ignorant reprobation of ancient Versions of the Book of God and by the introduction of a new one, released from the regulations which real learning prescribes, and

4. To convince him that our authorized Translators were fully prepared, and deficient in no respect, unto the good work which they undertook." (Todd, p. ix, x)

## The Organization of the Work

The quotes supporting the AV/KJB will be organized in the following way.

1. First, the quotes will be from authors whose lives were contemporary with the AV translators or shortly thereafter in the sixteen hundreds.

2. Second, quotes from the seventeen hundreds.

3. Third, quotes from the eighteen hundreds.

4. Fourth, quotes from the nineteen hundreds.

The quotes are secured from sources that are "not now of common occurrence" (Todd, *A Vindication of our Authorized Translation and Translators of the Bible*, p. iv).

# THE KJB'S ACCURACY & FAITHFULNESS

## Importance of Vernacular Translations

Some quotes are about the English translations prior to the AV. The reason relates to the instructions given to the translators from King James I of England.

King James I was described by many as a scholar. He was an intellectual. He was a linguist. His tutors had trained him in Biblical languages, such as Hebrew and Greek, as well as Latin and the prominent European languages of France and Spain. Shakespeare was his friend.

King James required the "fifty-four" AV/KJB translators to follow fifteen rules during their endeavor. The rules were issued through the Archbishop of Canterbury, Bishop Bancroft. Many copies of the rules were corrupted. However, Bishop Gilbert Burnett, a bishop and historian, received a reliable copy of "the King's instructions" from Dr. Thomas Ravis, one of the translators. Rule fourteen in Burnett's *History of the English Reformation* specifically says:

> "These Translations to be used, when they agree better with **the text** than the Bishops' Bible, viz. Tyndal's, Coverdale's, Mathewe's, Whitchurch's, Geneva." (Todd, p. 11). (my emphasis, HDW).

As we shall see, these English translations were based upon "**the text**" (see the quote above), which refers to the Hebrew, Aramaic, and Greek text. Today, the "texts" are known to us as the Hebrew Masoretic Text and the Greek Received Text. Therefore, the King James Bible followed the "original" *a priori*, as per the King's rules. Also, the King's instructions contained the

## INTRODUCTION

following important words found in rule number 1 and 2:

1. The ordinary Bible read in the Church, commonly called the Bishop's Bible, to be followed, and as little altered as *the truth of the original* will permit.

2. The names of the prophets and the holy writers, with the other names of the text, to be retained, as nigh as may be, accordingly as they were vulgarly used. (Burnett, as quoted by Todd, p. 9).

Note that the King's instructions refer to a **new translation** that follows the Bishop's Bible as well as other English versions. Most importantly, the translators were to follow a previous translation if **"the original will permit."**

Furthermore, the translators clearly stated in their "Preface" to the AV/KJB in 1611, under the heading, "The Purpose of the Translators, with their Number, Furniture, Care, etc.," the following:

> Truly (good Christian Reader) we never thought from the beginning, that we should need to make a new Translation, nor yet to make of a bad one a good one, (for then the imputation of Sixtus had been true in some sort, that our people had been fed with gall of Dragons instead of wine, with whey instead of milk:) but to make a good one better, or out of many good ones, one principal good one, not justly to be excepted against; that hath been our endeavor, that our mark. . . **If you ask what they had before them, truly it was the Hebrew text of the Old Testament, the Greek of the New.** These are the two golden pipes, or rather conduits, where-

# THE KJB'S ACCURACY & FAITHFULNESS

through the olive branches empty themselves into the gold. Saint Augustine calleth them precedent, or original tongues; Saint Jerome, fountains.

Therefore, there was a "fountain flowing" from the previous centuries that formed the *"foundation"* of the English Bibles. The "foundation" that the AV/KJB translators used was the "original" Hebrew Masoretic Text and the traditional Greek text, which goes by several names, but the most popular is the *Textus Receptus or* Received Text. Today, there are competing "original" texts that were "constructed" from corrupted manuscripts by men, rather than "received." The 54 translators rejected those manuscripts, because they knew that the heretics and cults had altered them.

The endeavor of the AV/KJB translators was "to make . . . out of many good ones (translations), one principal good one." They achieved their goal beyond measure! This is the 'testimony of history'!

## The Difficulties of Translating

John William Whittaker (1790?-1854), received his M.A. in 1817, B.D. in 1824, and D.D. in 1830. He was appointed examining chaplain by the Archbishop of Canterbury in 1819. It is said that his "learning was wide" (en.wikisource). His work, *"An Historical and Critical Inquiry into the Interpretation of the Hebrew Scriptures, with Remarks on Mr. Bellamy's New Translation,"* Cambridge, 1819 and Supplement, 1820, is well known. He was an Arabic scholar. He observes:

> "There are many passages, particularly in the Old Testament, of such acknowledged difficulty, that learned men never did, and perhaps never will, agree upon them. In these cases, if a

translator feel any uncertainty, his object ought to be the selection of that interpretation from former versions, which after mature consideration he thinks the best; nor would he be justified in forsaking them, unless *á priori* he had reason to believe that their authors were influenced by prejudice or the desire of supporting some favourite tenet. At any rate, it must be his duty to divest his mind of that ambitious tendency towards novelty, to which at some periods of life most critics are subject. A Translator must always incur great blame in adopting a new reading, and departing from the sense given by former interpreters, unless he could prove, at least *in foro conscientiae* (in favor of the conscience), that theirs was incorrect, and that his own gives the precise force which the inspired writer intended the words to bear. (Quarterly Review, London, May-June, 1820, Vol. XXIII, p. 292, p. 303 in the PDF; also see Todd, p. 40-41).

The translators of the AV/KJB achieved "one principal good one" and much, much more, as the comments and quotes to follow will testify. First, a brief look at those who opposed the AV/KJB.

## Quotes of Sciolists Opposed to the AV/KJB

A *sciolist* is a person who talks with pretended expertise, and as a result, displays sham learning that is designed to deceive or impress. Experts usually uncover them after a time. The real crime that occurs from sciolist activities is the tragic influence on the innocent. Victims of sciolists fill our churches. Frequently, they do not recover from the deceit of sciolists.

# THE KJB'S ACCURACY & FAITHFULNESS

Dr. J. W. Whittaker (q.v.) made the following comment related to sciolists and the AV/KJB. Please be aware that the use of the word "general" has changed over the centuries. By using the word "general," writers in the past meant "overall" or "complete." He said:

> The highest value has always been attached to our Translation of the Bible (AV/KJB). Sciolists, it is true, have often attempted to raise their own reputation on the ruin of that of others; and the authors of the English Bible have frequently been calumniated (falsely accused) by charlatans of every description: but it may safely be asserted, without fear of contradiction, that the nation at large has always paid our Translators the tribute of veneration and gratitude which they so justly merit. Like the mighty of former times, they have departed and shared the common fate of mortality; but they have not, like those heroes of antiquity, gone without their fame, though but little is known of their individual worth. Their reputation for learning and piety has not descended with them to the grave, though they are there alike heedless of the voice of calumny, and deaf to the praise which admiring posterity awards to the great and good. Let us not therefore too hastily conclude that they have fallen on evil days and evil tongues, because it has occasionally happened that *an individual, as inferior to them in erudition as in talents and integrity, is found questioning their motives, or denying their qualifications for the task which they so well performed.* Their Version has been used, ever since its first appearance, not only by the Church, but by all the sects which have forsaken her; and has justly been esteemed by all for its general

# INTRODUCTION

(overall, complete) **faithfulness,** and the severe beauty of its language. It has survived the convulsion both of Church and State, being universally respected by the enemies of both, when the Established Religion was persecuted with the most rancorous malignity; as if its merits were independent of circumstances, and left at a distance all the petty rivalships of sectarianism, and the effervescence of national frenzy. *It may be compared with any translation in the world, without fear of inferiority; it has not shrunk from the most rigorous examination; it challenges investigation; and, in spite of numerous attempts to supersede it, has hitherto remained unrivalled in the affections of the country.* (Todd, p. 80-81). (my bolding, HDW)

Over the years, the many false pretenses and claims of the critics, who are mostly sciolists, have led many students of the Bible, particularly the young, to the conclusion that the old English Bibles based upon the proper "original texts" are of **no authority.** Their conclusion is false. Nothing, and I repeat, NOTHING, could be farther from the Truth!

The major claim of *sciolists,* who are against the AV/KJB, is that the translation, as well as older English translations such as the Tyndale and Geneva Bibles, is not acceptable. Clement Cruttwell in an edition of the Bible, c. 1785, made the following comment about the claim of early sciolists against the English versions:

> It has been likewise a pretence, in this our day, that the ancient English Versions of the Bible are of no authority; and that the Translation of it now in use [the AV/KJB], like those which preceded it, is unfaithful to the Original. And

> therefore to me also it has been a gratifying employment, to bring forward abundant detections of the vanity and mischief of this **pretence**; and to select from such important guides, as I have named, whatever might promote my purpose. (Todd, p. 6) [my addition and emphasis, HDW]

This "pretence" is a tragedy and a wrongdoing that will surely be judged at the judgment seat of Christ (2 Corinthians 5:10).

## Examples of Sciolists

Lest the reader becomes wearied, or even doubtful, concerning sciolists who have written against the AV/KJB without examples being given, here are two from the last 400 years that are taken from many sources. There are many similar attacks in the present day literature.

## John Bellamy

In the history of false criticism of the AV/KJB, one of the most prominent condemners is John Bellamy, c. 1818. He acted as a committee of one to retranslate the Hebrew Scriptures. His scorn for the AV/KJB is well known. He claims the translators confined themselves to using primarily the Septuagint (LXX) and the Latin Vulgate. He said:

> It is allowed by the learned in this and in every Christian nation, that the authorized translations of the Sacred Scriptures, in many places, are not consistent with the original Hebrew. . . But it appears that they **confined** themselves to the Septuagint and the Vulgate; so

# INTRODUCTION

> that this was only working in the harness of the first translators; no translation having then been made from the original Hebrew only, for 1400 years. Indeed it was well known that there was **not** a critical Hebrew scholar among them; the Hebrew language, so indispensably necessary for the accomplishment of this important work, having been most shamefully neglected, in our Universities; and, as at this day, all candidates for orders were admitted without a knowledge of this primary, this most essential branch of Biblical learning. It was, as it is at present, totally neglected in our schools, and a few lessons taken from a Jew in term time, whose business it is to Judaize, and not to Christianize, serve to give the character of Hebrew scholars. (John Bellamy, *The Holy Bible Newly Translated from the Original Hebrew with Notes Critical and Explanatory*, Longman et al, London, 1818, p. i-ii, p. 15 in the PDF version). (my emphasis, HDW)

Of course, as we shall see, his statements are completely without confirmation and, not only that, they are false. However, what makes disagreeing with John Bellamy particularly difficult for this author is his own dislike of the Septuagint (LXX) and the Latin Vulgate. This author agrees with some of Mr. Bellamy's declarations concerning these texts. However, we must report that there are assertions by several qualified individuals, including the translators of the AV/KJB, that Jerome's translation from the Hebrew, the Latin Vulgate, was corrupted over the centuries (Todd, p. 101). Their claim is that the modern LXX text attributed to Jerome is not his. This author has not had time to investigate the truthfulness of these claims.

What is not amenable is Bellamy's acrid disagreement with the textual basis of the AV/KJB and his claims concerning the abilities of the fifty-four, more or less, translators (*v.s.*). Furthermore, he extracts quotes from authors that do not match their overall opinions concerning the AV/KJB translation [e.g. Bellamy's comments concerning Archbishop Newcome's opinions concerning the AV/KJB (see Todd, p. iv-v)]. There are authors today who do the same thing; their quotes are not contextual; they are taken out of context. Therefore, in this work, many of the quotes are purposefully long to avoid this travesty.

## A FALSE CLAIM

Many over the centuries have repeatedly questioned the skill of the AV/KJB translators to make a "new" translation. Mr. Bellamy is among the "many." This reveals another of Mr. Bellamy's faults, because the translators' contemporaries, as well as many scholars over the centuries, extol the abilities of the AV/KJB translators. John Hales (1584-1656), was a *contemporary* of the AV/KJB translators, who was "a most accomplished scholar." He said in 1617:

> The most partial for antiquity cannot choose but see and confess thus much, that for the literal sense *the interpreters of our own times, because of their skill in the original languages,* their care of pressing the circumstance and coherence of the text, and of comparing like places of Scripture with like, have generally surpassed the best of the ancients. (Todd, *An Authentic Account of Our Authorized Translation,* 2nd Edition, 1834, p. 12)

# INTRODUCTION

Contemporaries of Mr. Bellamy level some serious charges against his attitude and academic abilities. Rev. Clement Cruttwell in the early eighteen hundreds made the following comments:

> Of one of those persons, now maintaining the pretence [Bellamy's opinion that the AV/KJB "is unfaithful to the original"], I know nothing but his work; which has been strongly and too truly characterized, in a valuable pamphlet laid before me . . . 'an extreme irreverence for the Scriptures, shewn in the species of commentary which he has adopted, and the disputatious, contemptuous, unscriptural spirit with which it is conducted; in its ill-placed redundance of undigested verbal speculations, and it licentious departure from received interpretations of Scripture, and established doctrines'" (Todd, p. vi). (my addition, HDW)

Also, John Todd summarizes Rev. Cruttwell's additional comments, saying:

> The writer (Rev. C. Cruttwell) notices also, what is particularly to be observed, Mr. Bellamy's very **imperfect** knowledge of the Hebrew language, and incorrect use of the English; and announces a design to shew his Translation to be not what it professes to be, not translated from the Hebrew only, not an antidote to Deism, but a new text **for** Socinianism. (Todd, p. vii) (my emphasis, HDW)

In other words, Bellamy's text did not refute Deism as he claims in the preface to his work and on the title page of his work. Instead, his translation supports the heresy of Socinianism, which denies the deity of our Lord and Saviour, Jesus Christ.

If you are like this author, one wonders if Rev. Cruttwell and John Henry Todd's claims are accurate about Bellamy; especially since Bellamy had a contemporary, ardent supporter by the name of James Bland Burgess. After more research into Bellamy and Burgess, the conclusions of Cruttwell (sometimes spelled Crutwell) and Todd, which are quoted above, are undoubtedly correct.

For example, in the *Quarterly Review*, July, 1820, the following comments were made by J. W. Whittaker, M.A. Fellow of St. John's, Cambridge, concerning Bellamy's qualifications as well as his most ardent supporter, James Burgess. Whittaker said:

> In the first place, it appears that, whatever may be the present opinion of the public respecting Mr. Bellamy's qualifications, he has not yet been led to form a just estimate of them himself: for, notwithstanding all that has passed, he has published a second part of his translation in the same style with the first. In this he commits the same blunders; **displays the same ignorance of the plainest principles of Hebrew**; exhibits the same vulgar and incomprehensible jargon; repeats the same exploded falsehoods; and treats with the same insolence the learned persons who framed our present authorized translation. . . But, in the third place, we are now supplied with positive proof that, even after all which has passed, there is some danger of the public being led into the belief that Mr. Bellamy's translations are truly derived from the Hebrew, and that his charges

## INTRODUCTION

against the received version are not destitute of foundation. At least, there has appeared one individual who has publicly and unequivocally professed his belief in them—we allude to Sir James Bland Burgess, Bart. This gentleman, we understand, passes in certain circles for a literary character. We are well aware that this term is one of extensive signification, and is sometimes coupled with qualifications sufficiently humble.— Be this as it may, Sir James, as far as we are informed, has hitherto confined himself to works of imagination; in the present instance, however, he has attempted a more serious style of composition, and launched into the field of Biblical criticism. By what course of study he had prepared himself for such an effort, and by what or by whom he was deluded into the belief that he was qualified to enlighten the public mind in this department, must be left to the conjectures of the reader. (J. W. Whittaker, M.A. Fellow of St. John's; Cambridge, *Quarterly Review*, Vol. XXIII, March-July, 1820, "An Historical and Critical Enquiry into the Interpretation of the Hebrew Scriptures, with Remarks on Mr. Bellamy's New Translation," p. 287-288) (my bolding, HDW).

The *Quarterly Review* gives numerous "specimens" of Bellamy and Burgesses "blunders." Furthermore, it addresses their false claims:

1. "that there was not a single critical Hebrew scholar among the translators of the authorized version,"

2. that slander "all of the English Universities" then in existence, and

# THE KJB'S ACCURACY & FAITHFULNESS

3. "that all modern translations have been made from the Septuagint and Vulgate" (including the AV/KJB, HDW).

*The Quarterly Review,* No. 38, also addresses "Bellamy's Reply," saying:

> He [Mr. Bellamy] has no relish or perception of the exquisite simplicity of the Original, no touch of that fine feeling, that pious awe which led his venerable predecessors to infuse into their Version *as much of the Hebrew idiom, as was consistent with the perfect purity of our own* [English language]; a taste and feeling which have given perennial beauty and majesty to the English Tongue." (Todd, p. 80)

The Review also addresses Bellamy's "utter incompetency for the task he has undertaken" as well as the "plagiarism" of Burgess.

## Hugh Broughton

Others have attacked the AV/KJB translation, even during the time the translating of the AV/KJB was taking place. Remember, copies of the AV/KJB were sent for evaluation of the progress of translating to "divines" throughout the land.

A contemporary Hebrew scholar with an irascible personality severely demeaned the translation. The Hebraist was Hugh Broughton (1549-1612), fellow of Christ College, Cambridge. Several books and articles outline the reasons for his disdain of the translation. In brief, his old rival and an outstanding translator of the AV/KJB, John Rainolds (q.v), slighted him.

## INTRODUCTION

Furthermore, Broughton had pressed authorities for a 'new' English translation, a petition that was denied. However, his rival, Rainolds, secured permission for a new translation from King James I of England at the Hampton Court Conference. Broughton was particularly offended; especially, since the Bishop of Canterbury, Bancroft, did not invite him to participate in the translating endeavor. "Subsequently, he criticized the new translation unsparingly," as well as Bishop Bancroft, by writing a tract against him (en.wikipedia.org/wiki).

Dean John William Burgon addresses similar problems by unqualified translators that occurred in the ill-fated critical revision of the Received Text and production of the tainted *English Revised Version* (ERV) in 1885. Recall, this entire event is primarily the polluted work of B. F. Westcott and J. Fenton Hort. Burgon comments on the exclusion of heretics from the AV/KJB translation committees, but their inclusion in the ERV affair in the 1880's. He alludes to critics like Hugh Broughton. He said:

> Let it be further recollected that the greatest Scholars and the most learned Divines of which our Church could boast, conducted the work of Revision in King James' days; and it will be acknowledged that the promiscuous assemblage which met in the Jerusalem Chamber cannot urge any corresponding claim on public attention. **Then**, the Bishops of Lincoln of 1611, were Revisers: the Vance Smiths (a Unitarian) stood **without** and found fault. But in the affair of 1881, Dr. Vance Smith revises, and ventilates heresy from **within**: the Bp. of Lincoln stands outside, and is one of the severest Critics of the work.—

# THE KJB'S ACCURACY & FAITHFULNESS

> Disappointed men are said to have been conspicuous among the few assailants of our 'Authorized Version,'—Scholars (as **Hugh Broughton**) who considered themselves unjustly overlooked and excluded. (Burgon, *Revision Revised*, p. 513; p. 559 in the PDF). (my emphasis and addition, HDW)

In a current book by Paul D. Wegner, *Journey from Texts to Translations, The Origin and Development of the Bible*, he said:

> Another particularly virulent detractor was Dr. Hugh Broughton, a distinguished scholar who had not been asked to serve on the translation committee, most likely because his violent temper interfered with this ability to work well with others . . . Broughton's rejection of this new version was expected: "The late Bible . . . was sent to me to censure that will grieve me while I breathe, it is so ill done. Tell His Majesty that I had rather be rent in pieces with wild horses than any such translation by my consent should be urged upon poor churches. . . The new edition crosseth me. I require it to be burnt." (Paul D. Wegner, *Journey from Texts to Translations, The Origin and Development of the Bible*, Baker Academic, 1999, p. 313)

In addition, Todd relates:

> ...Hugh Broughton, fellow of Christ College, Cambridge; who had certainly attained great knowledge in the Hebrew and Greek tongues. But a more conceited or arrogant man hardly existed. With the Bishops' Bible he had found great fault; insisted upon the necessity of a new Translation; pronounced his own sufficiency to

## INTRODUCTION

make one exactly agreeable to the original text of the Hebrew; boasted of encouragement to this purpose from all ranks; and at length excited a very warrantable suspicion, that in so important a task, **he was unfit to be trusted**." (my emphasis, HDW)

Lastly, Broughton could not or did not document his objection to the AV/KJB translation then in progress. Dr. Brian Walton, "one of those most learned divines, who, **in 1656**, were publicly requested to consider the translations and impression of the Bible, and to offer their opinion therein to the Committee for Religion" (Todd, p. 68, footnote), said about Hebraist Hugh Broughton:

> "one, who being passed by, and not employed in the work, as one, though skilled in the Hebrew, yet of little or no judgment in that or any other kinde of learning, was so highly offended that he would needs undertake to shew *how many thousands places they had falsely rendered,* **when as he could hardly make good his undertaking in any one***!*" (my bolding and underlining, HDW)

Accounts like this are routinely found in the literature concerning those who would criticize the most accurate and faithful translation(s) into English of the Words *"given by inspiration of God."*

All too often, criticism of the AV/KJB translation is found in the religious literature from the sixteen hundreds up to and including modern times. Consistently, it is without merit.

Next, this work will present the support of our AV/KJB translation that has been blessed by God

# THE KJB'S ACCURACY & FAITHFULNESS

through the last 400 years. The quotes are from scholars who cannot be railed against.

McClure said:

> As to the Bible in its English form, it is safe to assume the impossibility of gathering a more competent body of translators, than those who did the work so well under King James's commission. (McClure, *The Translators Revived*, p. 232, p. 239 in the PDF).

# CHAPTER 1: QUOTES SUPPORTING THE AV/KJB TRANSLATION 1600s

## Richard Field, D.D.

Richard Field, D.D. (1561-1616), who was Dean of Gloucester in the early sixteen hundreds, wrote, *A View of the Controversies in Religion Which in These Last Times Have Caused the Lamentable Division in the Christian World.* Unfortunately, he died in 1616 before his multi-volume work was completed. He was one of the most admired preachers of the time. He was assembled with the others at the Hampton Court Conference where the decision was made by King James I to proceed with a new translation after the Puritan scholar, John Rainolds, suggested it.

Volume V of Dr. Fields work was not published before his death. Fortunately, several publishers subsequently published his materials. Another work was not published until 1716-1717. He had previously preached a sermon before the king at Whitehall, on Jude, verses 3-4, in London in 1604. Cattermole reports that Nathaniel Field, his son, published "a most valuable treatise" in 1628, which contained Dr. Field's sermon that was preached before the king. (Rev. Richard Cattermole, B.D., *The Literature of the Church of England Indicated in Selections from the Writings of Eminent Divines: With Memoirs of Their Live, and*

*Historical Sketches of the Times in Which They Lived*, Volume The First, 1844, p. 44). Dr. R. Field said the following:

> [I]t is by all agreed upon that all men by nature are strangers from the life of God, having their cogitations darkened in such sort that of themselves they cannot lift up their eyes to behold the brightness of that divine light, in the beholding whereof consisteth all their happiness; and that God, pitying this miserable estate of man, hath provided remedies against this evil, amongst which, that most excellent light of Christian Wisdom, revealed in the sacred books of the divine oracles is incomparable and peerless, as whereupon all other do depend, the bright beams of which heavenly light do shew unto us the ready way to eternal happiness, amidst the sundry turnings and dangerous wanderings of this life. And lest either the strangeness of the language wherein these holy books were written, or the deepness of the mysteries, or the multiplicity of hidden senses contained in them, should any way hinder us from the clear new and perfect beholding of that heavenly brightness; **God hath called and assembled into his Church out of all the nations of the world, and out of all people that dwell under the arch of heaven, men abounding in all secular learning and knowledge, and filled with the understanding of holy things, which might turn these scriptures and books of God into the tongues of every nation, and might unseal this book so fast clasped and sealed, and manifest and open the mysteries therein contained,** not only

# CHAPTER 1: QUOTES FROM THE 1600s

by lively voice, but by writings to be carried down unto all posterities. Good God! what treasure hath all the world comparable unto the treasure of those sacred books of God, and the writings, meditations, and happy marvels of the renowned worthies of the christian world? From hence, as from the pleasant and fruitful fields watered with the silver dew of Hermon, the people of God are nourished with all saving food. Hence the thirst of languishing souls is restinguished (quenched), as from the most pure fountains of living water, and the everlasting rivers of Paradise. Hence the want of needy souls is supplied, as out of the best and richest storehouse of the world. Hence: the soldiers of Christ are armed, as out of the best armoury, that they may be able to overthrow the, madness of infidels, and the fury of heretics. From hence, out of the school of all heavenly virtues, all the life, manners, and duties of men are framed and fashioned aright; the unlearned are taught, the learned are exercised; they that are fallen are holpen (helped), that they may be able to rise again; they that stand are preserved from the danger of falling. In a word, there is nothing honest, nothing profitable, pleasant, great, or rare and excellent, tending either to instruction, godliness of life, or the attaining of endless happiness, but here it may be found. (Cattermole, pp. 55-56; pp. 78-79 in PDF; Andrew McClure, *The Translators Revived*, 1855, pp. 224-225, pp. 231-232 in PDF; Todd, p. x, xi). (my addition, my emphasis, HDW)

This begins the journey through the last four centuries in celebration of the 400$^{th}$ anniversary of the AV/KJB. Without a doubt, great men of God with great

# THE KJB'S ACCURACY & FAITHFULNESS

abilities were gathered together in the early 1600's to translate the sacred 66 books of the Bible. They produced the most accurate and faithful translation into English to grace the face of the earth. It has not been matched. The praise for their work can be found in every century.

Lewis' *History of English Translations* in 1736 mentions the criticisms of the newly translated AV/KJB. However, he makes the following comment about some of the complaints. He said that they were:

> ". . . not exactly true." (Lewis, p. 330; p. 359 in the PDF)

This has been the case all too often in the history of translations. The enemy, in the form of sciolists, constantly bombards the public with conceited comments concerning certain translations. For example, even in these days, certain men and women attack the carefully made Spanish translation, the Reina Valera Gomez (RVG). Repeatedly, their narrow-mindedness is uncovered. Emanuel Rodriquez has written excellent articles relating to this topic, such as, "My Response to a Concerned Pastor Regarding the 1602 Valera "Purificada" Bible In Comparison to the RVG" and "Is Gail Riplinger right About the RVG." Brother Rodriquez is a missionary to Puerto Rico.

## Mr. Matthew Poole

John Lewis gives the following account recorded by Mr. Matthew Poole (1624 – 1679) from his *Synopsis Criticorum Biblicorum,* which is *a* 5 volume work from 1669-1675 in which he summarizes the views of one hundred and fifty biblical critics. The Old English in this quote was corrected to modern spelling.

# CHAPTER 1: QUOTES FROM THE 1600s

> "Of this Translation (the AV/KJB) the learned Mr. Matthew Poole has given the following character: 'In this Royal Version, says he, occur a good many Specimens of great Learning and Skill in the Original tongues, and of an Acumen and Judgment more than common'" (Lewis, p. 332; p. 361 in the PDF) (my addition, HDW).

Lewis also presents a quote from Tyndale's English translation of the New Testament from the "Prologue" to the Gospel of Matthew, which should be noted. This helps establish the long line of English translations preceding the AV/KJB that were dependent upon the "original" text in Hebrew, Aramaic, and Greek. Lewis said:

> Here, says he, hast thou, most dear reader, the New Testament or covenant made with us of God in Christ's blood, which I have looked over again (now at the last) with all diligence and compared it unto the Greke, and have weeded out of it many faults which lack of help at the beginning and oversight did sow therein. If ought seem changed, or not altogether agreeing with the Greke, let the finder of the fault consider the Hebrew phase or manner of speech left in the Greeke words, whose preterperfect tense and present tense is oft both one, and the future tense is the optative mode also, and oft the imperative mode in the active voice, and in the passive ever. Likewise person for person, number for number, and interrogation for a conditional and such like is with the Hebrew a common usage. (Lewis, p. 81).

This is the case for the English translations that follow Tyndale's Bible, such as the Matthew's Bible,

Whitchurch's (Cranmer's) Bible, Geneva Bible, and the Bishops' Bible. (see Todd, pp. 25-32).

## John Selden

John Selden (1584-1654) possessed "great oriental learning" (Todd, Index). He said:

> The English translation of the Bible is the best Translation in the world, and *renders the sense of the Original best*; taking in for the English Translation *The Bishops' Bible,* as well as King James's. The translators in King James's time took an excellent way. That part of the Bible was given to him, who was most excellent in such a tongue . . . then they met together, and one read the Translation, the rest holding in the hands some Bible, either the learned tongues, or French, Spanish, Italian, &c. If they found any fault, they spoke; if not, he read on . . . [T]he Bible is rather translated into English words than into English phrase. The Hebraisms are kept, and the phrase of that language is kept." (Todd, p. 68, 1819 Edition)

This is one of the methods that sealed the accuracy and faithfulness of the AV/KJB and for ever linked it to the original as no other version has EVER done.

## Brian Walton

Dr. Brian Walton (1600-1661) was an English scholar and English bishop. He was the primary mover in the publishing of the *Polyglot* Bible. In the *Polyglot* Bible "nine languages are used: Hebrew, Chaldee, Samaritan, Syriac, Arabic, Persian, Ethiopic, Greek and Latin. Among his collaborators were James Ussher, John Lightfoot and Edward Pococke, Edmund Castell,

# CHAPTER 1: QUOTES FROM THE 1600s

Abraham Wheelocke and Patrick Young, Thomas Hyde and Thomas Greaves." (en.wikipedia). Dr. Walton said:

> The last English Translation, made by diverse learned men at the command of King James, though it may justly contend with any now extant in any other language in Europe, was yet, carped and caviled at by diverse among ourselves; especially by one [Hugh Broughton], who being passed by, and not employed in the work, as one, though skilled in Hebrew, yet of little or no judgement [English spelling] in that or any other kinde of learning, was so highly offended that he would needs undertake to shew *how may thousand places they had falsely rendered, when as he could hardly make good his undertaking in any one!* (Todd, p. 69-70). [my additions, HDW].

## Ludwig Cappellus

Ludwig Cappellus (1585-1658), a German reformed theologian, was quoted by Dr. Edward Pococke (1604-1691), who was a celebrated Oxford Orientalist, Hebraist, and Biblical scholar. He is said to be "the best Arabick scholar that ever Europe produced." He supported Cappellus' statement (Todd, p. 70, 1819 Edition, footnote d).

The quote is long and there are run-on sentences. Nevertheless, it is the characteristic style of writing by scholars during those times. In the quote, the particularly important information is italicized.

> L. Cappellus saith, that translations are to be examined by the original text, if any copy of it be uncorrupted, and not that by translations: and

that is that therefore, which, not doubting those copies that we have to be so, I have endeavoured, in part, to do, so far at least as may serve *to justify, or to give account of, that Translation of our own which we follow; and deservedly; it being such and* **so agreeable to the Original,** *as that we might well choose among others to follow it, were it not our own, and established by authority among us;* which could not well be done without comparing it with others also, and bringing all to the original Hebrew, as the text, as hitherto it hath had the honour to be esteemed, and will so still have, having on it that divine impress, which will maintain its right and dignity against all that can be opposed. For the end proposed it was oft necessary to look into the signification of the words in that tongue, and what several senses they are capable of, that it may accordingly appear which of such, as by several interpreters are fastened on them, will be best agreeable to the place in which they occur, and according to the construction they are used in.—This having been observed by our Translators, *they have with great modesty and ingenuity, we see, put various readings or renderings in the margin of our Bibles,* as doubting which to prefer, and leaving it to the prudent reader which to choose; as if the one and the other were (as the Jews in such cases use to speak) *both the words of the living God;* both true and agreeable as well to the original words as to the analogy of faith. *And such modesty is by all in interpreting the Scriptures very imitable: and, being observed, would prevent many quarrels, in which the truth, by rashly contending for it, is lost, and such* *uncharitably censured as forsaking the truth, which did heartily seek it, and perhaps did not err from it.* (my bolding, HDW)

## AV/KJB Translators

The translators of the AV/KJB also defended their reliance on the "original sacred tongues," which are the Hebrew, Aramaic, and Greek, in their "Dedication" to King James. They wrote the following, which was published with the completed translation in 1611:

> For when Your Highness had once, out of deep judgment, apprehended how convenient it was, that, out of the Original sacred Tongues, together with comparing of the labours, both in our own and other foreign languages, of many worthy men who went before us, there should be one more exact translation of the Holy Scriptures into the English Tongue. . .

## The Translators Identified

The abilities of the translators are testimonies that help confirm, substantiate and corroborate the AV/KJB's accuracy and faithfulness to the original. The translators' scholarship, particularly in the area of languages, is unsurpassed. Several books extol the qualifications of the translators. For example, Alexander W. McClure's *The Translators Revived, Biographical Memoir of the Authors of the English Version of the Holy Bible*, which was published in 1853 by Charles Scribner, is well known. Also, Gustavus Paine's book, *The Men Behind The King James Version*, currently published by Baker House, is another good book. It was previously called *The Learned Men*, which was published in 1834. Laurence M. Vance has recently published a book that has valuable information called *King James, His Bible, and Its Translators.*

I have chosen to reproduce an earlier work on the translators than those mentioned above. The information concerning the translators is in a section from John Henry Todd's *A Vindication of Our Authorized Translation and Translators of the Bible*, first edition, 1819 and a third edition in 1838. The second edition was published in 1834. The section used was "Section VII" called "Of the translators of our authorized Bible. The learning of their time." The first part of this section is from Todd's first edition and the second part is from his third edition. I have placed it in an appendix on page 85. Please note that the 'footnotes' have been moved to 'endnotes.' Todd's footnotes are alphabetized, instead of numbered.

# CHAPTER 2: QUOTES SUPPORTING THE AV/KJB TRANSLATION 1700s

## Jonathan Swift

Jonathan Swift (1667-1775), also known as Dean Swift, was Dean of St. Patrick's, Dublin, in 1713. In a letter to the Earl of Oxford called "A Proposal For Correcting, Improving and Ascertaining The English Tongue" from London on February 22, 1711, He praised the AV/KJB. He said:

> It is your Lordship's observation, that if it were not for the Bible and Common Prayer Book in the vulgar tongue, we should hardly be able to understand any thing that was written among us an hundred years ago; which is certainly true: for those books being perpetually read in Churches, have proved a kind of standard for language, especially to the common people. And I doubt, whether the alterations since introduced [in language] have added much to the beauty or strength of the English tongue, though they have taken off a great deal from that simplicity, which is one of the greatest perfections in any language. You, my Lord, who are so conversant in the Sacred Writings, and *so great a judge of them in their originals,* will agree *that no Translation our country ever yet produced, hath come up to that of the Old and New Testament;*

> *and by the many beautiful passages, which I have often had the honour to hear your Lordship cite from thence, I am persuaded that the Translators of the Bible were masters of an English style much fitter for that work, than any we see in our present writings;* which I take to be owing to the simplicity that runs through the whole."
> (http://ebooks.adelaide.edu.au/s/swift/jonathan/s97p/, also see Todd, p. 74).

## Alexander Geddes

Alexander Geddes, LL.D., (1737-1802) was a Scottish theologian and scholar. He was author of *Critical Remarks on the Hebrew Scriptures: corresponding with a new Translation of the Bible.* He had the following to say about the AV/KJB:

> The highest eulogiums have been made on the Translation of James the First both by our own writers, and by foreigners. **And indeed, if accuracy, fidelity, and the strictest attention to the letter of the text, be supposed to constitute the qualities of an excellent Version, this of all Versions, must, in general, be accounted the most excellent.** Every sentence, every word, every syllable, every letter and point, seem to have been weighed with the nicest exactitude, and expressed either in the text, or margin, with **the greatest precision**. Pagninus himself is hardly more literal; and it was well remarked by Robertson, above a hundred years ago, *that it may serve for a Lexicon of the Hebrew language, as well as for a Translation.* (Todd, p. 75) (my emphasis, HDW).

# CHAPTER 2: QUOTES FROM THE 1700s

## Samuel Horsley

Dr. Geddes' work was reviewed in 1794 in a contemporary journal of that age by a person thought to be Samuel Horsley (1733-1806), Bishop of Rochester, who said:

> When the translators in James the first's time began their work, they prescribed to themselves some rules, which it may not be amiss for all translators to follow. *Their reverence for the Sacred Scriptures induced them to be as literal as they could*, to avoid obscurity; and it must be acknowledged, that they were extremely happy in the simplicity and dignity of their expressions. *Their adherence to the Hebrew idiom is supposed at once to have enriched and adorned our language;* and as they laboured for the general benefit of the learned and the unlearned, they avoided all words of Latin original, when they could find words in their own language, even with the aid of adverbs and prepositions, which would express their meaning. Therefore, *make* is better than *constitute*; and *look into* is better than *inspect.* Another rule they adopted was, to exclude technical expressions. Instead of *cavalry,* they put *horsemen*; instead of *muster,* they put *number.* In this there was a dignity, *a superior reverence to the Word of God.* The revival of learning introduced a practice of transposing words, from their grammatical order, into an order somewhat resembling the Greek and Roman. In this respect too they consulted the genius of our own language, which rarely admits of such a transposition. (Todd, p. 76)

Commenting in the preface to his translation of Hosea, Samuel Horsley made the following humble comment:

> With respect to my translation, I desire that it may be distinctly understood, that I give it not as one that ought to supersede the use of the Public Translation (AV/KJB) in the service of the Church. (my addition, HDW).

## Dr. Robert Gray

Dr. Gray (1762-1834), Bishop of Bristol, was a respected scholar and Hebraist. He wrote *The Key to the Old Testament*, which went through at least nine editions. There is a detailed history about Dr. Gray in *The Annual Biography and Obituary, Vol 19*, 1835, pages 258-264. He said the following in his book, *The Key*:

> The Romanists made many unreasonable objections against this translation; and the Presbyterian professed themselves dissatisfied. It was however allowed, even by Cromwell's committee, to be the best extant, and certainly it is a most wonderful and incomparable work, equally remarkable for the general **fidelity** of its construction, and the magnificent simplicity of its language. (Dr. Robert Gray, *The Key to the Old Testament*, 1792, p. 32; p. 51 in PDF) (my emphasis, HDW; remember "general" means complete or overall in the past)

In another place, Dr. Gray said this:

> Every sincere and well-disposed admirer of the Holy Oracles may be satisfied with the present Translation, which is, indeed, highly

excellent; being in its doctrines uncorrupt, and in its general construction **_faithful to the Original._** (Todd, p. 75; He reports the quote from a second edition of The Key to the Old Testament, 2$^{nd}$ Introduction, p. 43).

In spite of Dr. Gray's predilection for "new" discoveries of manuscripts, he was sincere and honest in his approach to the texts used by the AV/KJB translators. In retrospect, we can report that most of the "new" manuscripts discovered, after the Reformation, were severely corrupted and contained only portions of the various books of the Bible.

## Robert Lowth

Robert Lowth (1710-1787) was Oxford Professor of Poetry and the author of one of the most influential textbooks of English grammar (en.wikipedia). In the second edition of his grammar book, he said this about the AV/KJB:

> The Vulgar translation of the Bible—is the best standard of our language.

And the AV/KJB shall always be so, because it is so wonderfully tied to the "original" "God-breathed" Words. And, it is translated in such a way that it will never be surpassed because of its simplicity of phrasing, beauty of words, preciseness, accuracy, faithfulness, and standard of translating.

# CHAPTER 3: QUOTES SUPPORTING THE AV/KJB TRANSLATION 1800s

## Quarterly Review

In an article on "Liturgical Reform" in the *Quarterly Review* published in 1834, an interesting account was located. The article was concerned with the Anglican *Psalter* (Psalms) in the Anglican *Prayer Book*, which was considered a paraphrase by many (rather than a literal translation).

> Mr. Cox and Mr. Riland declare their entire assent to the following judgment of Dr. (Adam) Clarke (*q.v.*): The Psalms in the Prayer Book are rather a ***paraphrase*** than a version. There are many words, turns of thought, and varieties of mood, tense, and person in it which do not appear in the others. In the Psalms in our **authorized (AV/KJB) version**, the translators conscientiously, where they have added anything, even the smallest particle to fill up the sense, or to accommodate the Hebrew idiom to that of the English, have, shown this by putting the expletive word in the *Italic* letter. Thousands of such expletives—many of them utterly unnecessary—are to be found in the Psalms in the Prayer Book, but they have *there* no such distinguishing mark, and are all printed as if they

were the words of the Holy Spirit. Clarke ap. Cor, p. 55. (my addition, HDW)

David Norton, editor of *The New Cambridge Paragraph Bible, With The Apocrypha, King James Version,* which was published in 2005 by Cambridge University Press, is a recent popular edition of the Bible. I have collated several of the New Testament books with the Cambridge Defined King James Bible published by Bible For Today. Norton's edition has **no** italicized words. This is a travesty.

Although the author of the article in the *Quarterly Review,* mentioned above, is uncertain and although he did not favor Dr. Clarke's opinion, he penned the following note:

> "Nothing could be more right and proper than the making, in the reign of James I that wonderful Translation of the Bible—**wonderful** both **for purity of language and accuracy of interpretation.**" ("Liturgical Reform," *Quarterly Review,* Jan., 1834, p. 541; also in Todd's 3rd Edition)

## Thomas Rennell, D.D.

Thomas Rennell (c. 1754-1840) was appointed the Dean of Winchester in 1805. In 1798, he was given the title, Master of the Temple, which was one of the two titles given to Anglican Clergy; the other title was "Reader of the Temple." "He was noted as a profound Greek scholar" (John Nichols, *Literary Anecdotes of the Eighteenth Century,* p. 729). Dr. Rennell was mentioned in *The Anti-Jacobin, or, Weekly Examiner,* a newspaper founded by George Canning in 1797. A Jacobin was an Englishman and member of a club dedicated to

## CHAPTER 3: QUOTES FROM THE 1800s

centralized, governmental power. Thomas Rennell's sermons were mentioned in a very positive light in 1815 in *The Anti-Jacobin,* Volume IX. His comments demonstrated that the **"new"** translations of his time were for promoting the heresy of Socinianism and other devious heresies. Rennell said:

> From either of these schemes, the bold project of a new Translation, or the more specious one of a Revisal of the present Version of the Holy Scriptures (AV/KJB), there can be so little gained, and may be so much hazarded, that the probable good bears no manner of proportion to the threatened danger. We have indeed specimens of new Versions both of the whole, and various parts, of the Old and New Testaments; some of them, particularly of the Old Testament, clearly intended as a vehicle for loose and licentious speculation. The language of the New Testament is distorted in violation of all analogy of sense and diction, to speak the opinion of Socinus (Socinianism).

> But even the best of these specimens, executed by men of acknowledged talents and soundness of opinion, recommend most strongly, *by their avowed inferiority in every essential point, an adherence to that we are already in possession of.* (In other words, there was no need for changing the accurate, faithful AV/KJB). With regard to a revision, it is of little importance that a few particles be adjusted, a few phrases polished, if the whole fabric of that faith **<u>which was once delivered to the saints</u>** is thereby shaken to its foundations. For the extent and progress of such a revision, or the objects it may

embrace, no man who is acquainted can at all calculate.

With regard to the New Testament, I am sure we may confidently affirm (Rennell was a Greek scholar), that, in a well known instance, the industry, learning, and abilities which have been sedulously exerted in collecting the mistakes and inaccuracies, **which are said to exist** in the received Version (AV/KJB), have scarcely been able to produce a single error, by which any material fact, or doctrine, is affected. Add to this, that the grandeur, dignity, and simplicity of it is confessed even by those, who wish eagerly to promote a revision of it; and by the most eminent critics, and masters of style, it is allowed to exhibit a more perfect specimen of the integrity of the English language, than any other writing which that language can boast.

But the grounds, on which these projects are to be resisted, are much more serious and important. For when we see men of the most latitudinarian principles (i.e., tolerant of variations in doctrine) uniformly pressing forward this dangerous proposal; when we see the most unbounded panegyrics (extravagant praise delivered in formal speech or writing) bestowed on those, who have converted the Mosaic history into allegory, and the New Testament in Socinianism, when we see these attempts studiously fostered, and applauded, by the advocates for this projected revision; we must conjecture, that something more is meant than a correction of mistakes, or an improvement of diction. Those doctrines, the demolition of which we know to be, in late instances, the grand object of such innovators when they propose alteration in articles of faith, or correction of liturgical forms, are surely in still greater danger when attempted, by the same men, under the distant approaches of a revision of our English Bible. (Todd, p. 78-80). (my additions, HDW).

## Thomas Fanshawe Middleton

Thomas Middleton (1769-1822) was Bishop of Calcutta, India, who founded Bishops' College in Calcutta. He is known for his book on the Greek article. There is an ebook, *The Life of Thomas Fanshawe Middleton*, available, which extols the accomplishments of this missionary and scholar.

Middleton said:

> The style of our present Version (AV/KJB) is incomparably superior to any thing which might be expected from the finical (demanding, exacting, finicky) and perverted taste of our own age. It is simple, it is harmonious, it is energetic; and, which is of no small importance, use has made it familiar, and time has rendered it sacred.

## Dr. Adam Clarke

Dr. Adam Clarke (1760-1832) was "a profound Oriental scholar," author of a *Commentary on the Bible*, and editor of a collection of state papers supplementary to Rymer's *Federa*. (Robert Chambers, Cyclopedia of English Literature, Vol. II, 1856, p. 660). Dr. Clarke was also a participant in the effort to produce a "new" "London Polyglot" Bible. In 1810, Dr. Clarke published *A Prospectus of his Intended Edition of the Old and New Testaments, with Notes,* and the first part was produced

## THE KJB'S ACCURACY & FAITHFULNESS

in 1810 (*An Account of the Religious and Literary Life of Adam Clarke,* LL.D., F.A.S., Vol. I, 1837, p. 394). He was well qualified to make the following comment(s):

> Those who have compared most of the European Translations with the original, have not scrupled to say, that the English Translation of the Bible, made under the direction of King James the first, is the most **accurate and faithful** of the whole. Nor is this its only praise; the Translators have seized the very spirit and soul of the **Original**, and expressed this almost every where, with pathos and energy. Besides, our translators have not only made a standard Translation; but they have made their Translation the standard of our language: the English tongue in their day was not equal to such a work— "but God enabled them to stand as upon mount Sinai," to use the expression of a learned friend, "and crane up their country's language to the dignity of the **originals**, so that after the lapse of 200 years, the English Bible is, with very few exceptions, the standard of the purity and excellence of the English tongue. The **Original** from which it was taken, is, alone, superior to the Bible translated by the authority of King James." This is an opinion, in which my heart, my judgment and my conscience coincide." (Adam Clarke, LL.D. *The Holy Bible Containing the Old and New Testaments: The Text Carefully Printed From the Most Correct Copies of the Present Authorized Translation. Including the Marginal Readings and Parallel Texts. With the Commentary and Critical Notes, Designed as a Help to a Better Understanding of The Sacred Writings,* Vol. I, NY, 1811, p. xxi)

# CHAPTER 3: QUOTES FROM THE 1800s

Furthermore, Dr. Clarke said this about King James I, who has been so maligned over the last 400 years by far too many:

> The Character of James the *First* has been greatly under rated. In the Hampton-Court Conference, he certainly shewed a clear and ready comprehension of every subject brought before him; extensive reading, and remarkably sound judgment. **For the *best Translation* into any language**, we are indebted under God to King James, who was called a *hypocrite* by those who had no *religion*; and a *pedant* by person who had not half his *learning*. Both piety and justice require, that while we are thankful to God for the gift of his word, we should revere the memory of the man, who was the instrument of conveying the water of life, through a channel by which its purity has been so wonderfully preserved. (Clarke, p. xxi).

In addition, Dr. Clarke said:

> "There have been many translations of the Old and New Testaments, but *the best ever made, take it in the whole, is that in common use, first published in* 1611, commonly called King James's Bible, because published by royal authority. For accuracy, and general fidelity, competent judges allow, that this Translation greatly exceeds all modern versions, either English or foreign (Clarke, *View of Sacred Literature*, published in 1830, p. 88.)

## Dean John William Burgon

Dean John William Burgon (1813-1888), Dean of Chichester, was a noted scholar (Dr. and Mrs. D. A.

# THE KJB'S ACCURACY & FAITHFULNESS

Waite, "Who Was Dean John William Burgon?" http://www.deanburgonsociety.org/DeanBurgon/whowasdb.htm). He was offended that "revisionists" in the mid to late eighteen hundreds desired to revise the AV/KJB. The revision, called *The English Revised Version,* was based upon a 'fabricated' or constructed text. Dean Burgon said:

> It follows that, in our account, the 'New English Version,' has been all along a foredoomed thing. If the 'New Greek Text' be indeed a tissue of fabricated Readings, the translation of these into English must needs prove lost labour. It is superfluous to enquire into the merits of the English rendering of words which Evangelists and Apostles demonstrably never wrote. Even this, however, is not nearly all. As Translators, full two-thirds of the Revisionists have shown themselves singularly deficient,—alike in their critical acquaintance with the language out of which they had to translate, and in their familiarity with the idiomatic requirements of their own tongue. They had a noble Version before them, which they have contrived to spoil in every part. Its dignified simplicity and essential faithfulness, its manly grace and its delightful rhythm, they have shown themselves alike unable to imitate and unwilling to retain. Their queer uncouth phraseology and their jerky sentences :—their pedantic obscurity and their stiff, constrained manner: their fidgetty affectation of accuracy,—and their habitual achievement of English which fails to exhibit the spirit of the original Greek ;—are sorry substitutes for the living freshness, and elastic freedom, and habitual fidelity of the grand old Version which we

## CHAPTER 3: QUOTES FROM THE 1800s

inherited from our Fathers, and which has sustained the spiritual life of the Church of England, and of all English-speaking Christians, for 350 years. Linked with all our holiest, happiest memories, and bound up with all our purest aspirations: part and parcel of whatever there is of good about us: fraught with men's hopes of a blessed Eternity and many a bright vision of the neverending. Life;—the Authorized Version, wherever it was possible, should have been jealously retained . . . Bishop Ellicott has [said]: " No Revision" (he says) "in the present day could hope to meet with an hour's acceptance if it failed to preserve the tone, rhythm, and diction of the present Authorized Version." (Dean John William Burgon, *Revision Revised*, pp. 225-226; pp. 271-272 in the PDF version) [my addition, HDW]

Dean Burgon excoriates the choices of the "Revisionists" as they translated the "quote-unquote" Greek "Received Text." In reality, the text was revised or reconstructed by the revisers and became the basis of the modern critical text known as the *United Bible Society's Text* (UBS) or *Nestle-Aland Text* (NA) (now called the $UBS^4$, published by the American Bible Society or $NA^{27}$, now in its $27^{th}$ edition, published by the German Bible Society). Burgon said:

We turn to the place indicated, and are constrained to assure these well-intentioned men, that the phenomenon we there witness is absolutely fatal to their pretensions as ' Revisers' of our Authorized Version. Were it only some passing difficulty which their method occasions us, we might have hoped that time would enable us to overcome it. But since it is the genius of the

> English language to which we find they have offered violence; the fixed and universally-understood idiom of our native tongue which they have systematically set at defiance; the matter is absolutely without remedy. The difference between the A. V. (Authorized Version) and the R. V. (Revised English Version) seems to ourselves to be simply this,—that the renderings in the former (the Authorized Version) are the idiomatic English representations of certain well-understood Greek tenses: while the proposed substitutes are nothing else but the pedantic efforts of mere grammarians to reproduce in another language idioms which it abhors. (Burgon, *Revision Revised*, pp. 204-205 in the PDF version) (my additions, HDW)

And:

> Not the least service which the Revisionists have rendered has been the proof their work affords, how very seldom our Authorized Version is materially wrong: how faithful and trustworthy, on the contrary, it is throughout. (Burgon, *Revision Revised*, p. 232; p. 278 in the PDF)

Moreover, the following quote notes the all-too-often lax printing by "stationers," printers authorized by the government in England for centuries, who frequently made many printing errors. However, in the early years following the development of the printing press in 1450 A.D., printing methods remained unsophisticated. Dean Burgon said:

> The cheapest copies of our Authorized Version at least exhibit the Word of GOD **faithfully** and helpfully. Could the same be said of a cheap edition of the work of the Revisionists

... (Burgon, *Revision Revised*, p. 513, p. 559 in the PDF) (my emphasis, HDW)

D. A. Waite, Th.D., Ph.D., has noted Dean Burgon's stand concerning the AV/KJB, saying:

> The Authorized (King James) Version was found by Dean Burgon to be far superior in every way to any other version of his day. By extension, similar arguments might be made against the false versions of our own day. (D. A. Waite, Th.D., Ph.D., *Westcott and Hort's Greek Text and Theory Refuted, Summarized From Dean Burgon's Revision Revised*, p. App. 4 in an appendix to *Revision Revised* by the Dean Burgon Society, p. 602 in the PDF).

## Solomon Caesar Malan

From his earliest youth, Solomon Caesar Malan (1812-1894) manifested a remarkable faculty for the study of languages, and when he came to Scotland as tutor in the marquis of Tweeddale's family at the age of 18 he had already made progress in Sanskrit, Arabic and Hebrew (en.wikipedia). He was vicar of Broadwindsor. He published *A Vindication of the Authorized Version, from Charges Brought Against it by Recent Writers* in 1856 and *A Plea for the Received Greek Text and for The Authorised Version of The New Testament in answer to Some of the Dean of Canterbury's Criticisms on Both*.

The following is from David Cloud's, *For Love of the Bible, The Battle for the King James Version and the Received Text from 1800 to Present,* Way of Life Literature, 2nd Edition, 1999, pp. 96-100 and the emphasis is by Brother Cloud in Malan's quote.

## THE KJB'S ACCURACY & FAITHFULNESS

"It [the KJV] **stands as yet unrivalled among other modern versions** for the devout spirit in which its authors rendered the original texts; for the simple beauty of its style; and for the dignified and easy flow of a language that was in a great degree formed from it, and that singles it out from among other translations of the Bible, even as a mere literary composition. It is free from the ruggedness and from the archaisms of the older English versions; and at the same time it possesses at least an equal merit with them, for its faithful rendering of the original. But **it has this great advantage over some of them, that whereas they were the work of single individuals, this was made by a goodly company of nearly fifty of the most pious and learned men of that time; who, together, availed themselves of the labours of their predecessors in order to raise their own production to a higher degree of excellence.**

"**It may, indeed, be taken down; but, if so, never to be rebuilt as it was. It might, it is true, have a more modern appearance; but then, it would lose the solemn look of age. It might also possibly be better adapted to the fastidious taste of the present day; but then, unbroken associations of two centuries and a half, together with much of national individuality, would perish for ever; and those persons who think the Authorized Version antiquated** (words in the KJV)" , **would be the first to regret the change**. ... And they would lament the day when, for the sake of novelty, they had abandoned those sweet and solemn words of warning blended with their earliest

# CHAPTER 3: QUOTES FROM THE 1800s

recollections of childhood, by renouncing their trust of a national treasure, committed to them in the safe keeping of the Authorized English Version of the Bible. ...

"So much care, so much earnestness, in the due performance of this important task [the creation of the King James Bible], were not bestowed in vain. **They have stamped the work with a character for excellence to which no modern version, and but one or two of the older ones, can lay claim.** As regards the Old Testament, the Authorized Version is, generally speaking, less paraphrastic, and is therefore a more correct rendering of the Hebrew, than the Septuagint and the versions that follow them wholly or in part; such as the Armenian, the Ethiopic, the Coptic, the Vulgate, the Arabic, and even the Syriac. ... And, as regards the New Testament, the English Bible agrees best with the old versions, which are of the highest value, on account of their faithfulness and accuracy...

"**[I]t stands pre-eminent when side by side with more modern versions,—not only for its devout adherence to the original texts, but also for the beauty of its style.** ... So true is this, that whereas neighbouring nations have had, within a short period, a succession of versions of the Bible in their respective languages, to the detriment of union and of uniformity among the readers of the Bible in those countries, the English Version has stood on its own merits, and has shone of its own lustre for nearly two centuries and a half. ...

"Thus it is that it has entered into the very substance of the nation. It is interwoven with its

# THE KJB'S ACCURACY & FAITHFULNESS

sinews, and forms more than any other book ever did—an unseen, by many perhaps, unacknowledged, or even neglected, but still a living, element in the prosperity of the people. ... **THESE LASTING AND WHOLESOME EFFECTS ARE THE RESULT OF THE ENGLISH BIBLE BEING ONE AND THE SAME FOR ALL. IF, INSTEAD OF ONLY ONE BIBLE, ENGLAND HAD, LIKE SOME OTHER COUNTRIES, MANY BIBLES, THAT VARIETY ALONE WOULD BREED AND FOSTER ENDLESS DIVISION.** ...

"Their reverence for the Sacred Scriptures induced them [KJV translators] to be as literal as they could, to avoid obscurity; and it must be acknowledged that they were extremely happy in the simplicity and dignity of their expressions. Their adherence to the Hebrew idiom is supposed at once to have enriched and adorned our language; and, as they laboured for the general benefit of the learned and the unlearned, they avoided all words of Latin original when they could find words in their own language ...

"Thus, then, the English Bible has not only stood for centuries, and **NOW STANDS, ON ITS OWN MERITS AS A TRUE WITNESS OF THE INSPIRED TEXT OF SCRIPTURE**; but it is also strong of its own strength, in being, as the highest authorities tell us, 'the best standard of the English language.' ... **For 'our translators,' says Dr. Adam Clarke, 'not only made a standard translation, but they have made their translation the standard of our language. THE ENGLISH TONGUE, IN THEIR DAY, WAS NOT EQUAL TO SUCH A WORK; BUT GOD**

## CHAPTER 3: QUOTES FROM THE 1800s

**ENABLED THEM TO STAND AS UPON MOUNT SINAI, AND CRANE UP THEIR COUNTRY'S LANGUAGE TO THE DIGNITY OF THE ORIGINALS,** so that after the lapse of two hundred [and fifty] years, the English Bible is, with very few exceptions, the standard of the purity and excellence of the English tongue. The original, from which it was taken, is alone superior to the Bible translated by the authority of King James ...

"Such considerations, however, have no weight whatever with many who are willing to sacrifice much to the love of change; or at all events, who seem to take pleasure in aiming blows at everything that is not of yesterday. **Everything now must keep pace with the age; even the word of God.** ... And yet wisdom neither came with us, nor will die with us. As regards the Authorized Version then, and those who find fault with it, 'let us not too hastily conclude,' says Mr. Whittaker, 'that the translators have fallen on evil days and evil tongues, because **it has occasionally happened that an individual, as inferior to them in erudition as in talents and integrity, is found questioning their motives, or denying their qualifications for the task which they so well performed.** ... **It [the KJV] may be compared with any translation in the world, without fear of inferiority; it has not shrunk from the most rigorous examination; it challenges investigation**; and, in spite of numerous attempts to supersede it, it has hitherto remained unrivalled in the affections of the country.'

"And God grant it may long continue so, for the good of the people to which it belongs! ...

"I purpose therefore ... to look into the charges thus brought forward against the English Bible, with those who cling to it as they ought, affectionately and devoutly; in order to assist them in expelling from their mind all doubt on the subject. Meanwhile, **they may rest assured that, hitherto, all attempts at improvement upon their Bible, have come far short of it in language, in style, in truthfulness, and above all, in a generally correct and devout rendering of the origi**nal texts" (Malan, *A Vindication*, pp. i-xvi, xxii-xxvi).

Malan answered the various arguments that were being put forth in advance of a revision of the Authorized Version. For example:

"... we now hear from many, that the English Bible is no longer suited to the exigencies of the present day, but that our advanced state of knowledge loudly calls for a new revision. An evil day that will be when it comes. However, Bishop Middleton holds out no encouragement to them, when he says: 'The **style of our present version is incomparably superior to anything which might be expected from the finical and perverted taste of our own age.** It is simple, it is harmonious, it is energetic; and, which is of no small importance, use has made it familiar, and time has rendered it sacred.' ... its words are 'household words,' ... its simple and hallowed language is understood and loved alike, by the poor peasant and by the august Sovereign, whom it binds to Her people. **England has not 'a Bible,' one of many to choose from, like her**

## CHAPTER 3: QUOTES FROM THE 1800s

**neighbours; but 'the Bible' is in every English home; and 'my Bible,' in English, means that *one* Book, the very words of which are the same for all"** (Malan, *A Vindication*, pp. xviii, xix).

Malan plainly saw the danger of loosing from the ancient moorings of the Received Text and the Authorized Version.

"Who will be bold, or I might almost say hardened enough, if not perhaps to pull down, yet even to whitewash the stately edifice of the English Bible? ... It might possibly be better adapted to the fastidious taste of the age; but then, unbroken associations of two centuries and a half, together with much of national individuality, would perish for ever; and those persons who think the authorized version antiquated would be the first to regret the change. ... For independently of the words of the Bible being sacred in all languages, the language of the English Bible in particular is consecrated ... the vernacular translation of the Bible has formed and fixed the language of the country" (Malan, *A Vindication of the Authorized Version*, 1856, pp. iii, iv, xiv).

Malan pointed out the unsettled, ever-changing character of modern textual criticism, observing: "In other words, the translator chooses his own text, which he renders as he thinks fit; so that, in fact, he has it all his own way. ... Mill is thought by some to be antiquated, Griesbach out of date, and Tischendorf even not exactly to their taste" (Malan, *A Vindication of the Authorized Version*, p. xxi).

## THE KJB'S ACCURACY & FAITHFULNESS

Malan "takes exceptions even to the quite prevalent custom of ministers' criticising the present translation before their congregations, on the ground that it 'needlessly unsettles the mind of their hearers on a subject in which comparatively few of them can ever be fair judges'" (Bissell, *The Historic Origin of the Bible*, p. 350).

In the second book, Malan directed his remarks to a critique of Henry Alford's sixth edition Greek New Testament (published in 1868) which followed Tischendorf and gave heavy preference to the Vaticanus and Sinaiticus manuscripts. Malan comments on some of Alford's readings in the Gospels and the book of Titus. The following two examples illustrate the tone of the whole:

"[Matthew 1:25] 'Till she had brought forth her first-born son,' A.V. is changed by Dr. Alford to 'till she had brought forth a son'! His reasons for this change are, that the Vatican MS. and a very few others make it; whereas the reading of the Auth. Version, which is that of the Received Text , is far better supported, and by many more MSS. The English reader may refer to p. 37 for a discussion on this passage; but if he knows no Greek, he may rest assured the Authorized Version is right and far better than the Dean's alteration 'till she brought forth *a son*'..." (Malan, *A Plea for the Received Text and for the Authorized Version of the New Testament*, p. 103).

"[Mark 13:14] 'Spoken of by Daniel the prophet,' A.V., 'omit,' Dr. Alford. This clause is not, indeed, in the Vatican MS., but is found in

## CHAPTER 3: QUOTES FROM THE 1800s

others, as well as in the Syriac, Georgian, Slavonic, and Ethiopic versions. So that we need not obey Dr. Alford's peremptory order to omit it" (Ibid., p. 142).

Malan's conclusion offers a window into the sympathies of a great many nineteenth-century preachers toward the attempts to undermine the Greek Received Text:

**"A man who, like him [Henry Alford], sets to a work of this kind, apparently without the slightest hesitation or misgiving in his own powers, thinking it the easiest thing in the world to make wholesale changes in the Greek text and in the joint labours of more than fifty learned men of old, instead of dealing with the utmost reverence and caution, not only forms an unworthy estimate of the work he undertakes—but he also recklessly wounds the feeling of deep respect and affection with which men, nowise his inferiors in judgment or scholarship, still continue to look upon the Received Text and the English Bible.**

"Both these have, indeed, lasted more than two centuries; a long time, in truth, for those who think that wisdom, learning, and scholarship have only just dawned on the land, and that, until now, all was darkness and ignorance. Wise men, however, do not think so but rather take the long life of those two monuments of ancient piety and learning as a proof of their real merit and excellence. ...

"[A] better acquaintance with his [Alford's] work only tends to deepen their reverence and to strengthen **their affection for their old friends and companions, the Received Greek Text of the New Testament and the Authorised Version of it—neither of which they ever intend to give up**; not even at the Dean's bidding" (Malan, *A Plea for the Received Text and for the Authorized Version of the New Testament*, pp. 210, 11).

When the 1881 English Revision appeared, Malan was not swayed from his earlier position. "The learned writer charged the Revisers with having 'looked upon' their work 'in the light of a Greek exercise,' and with having 'taken pleasure in making as many changes as they could, with little or no regard for cadence, rhythm, style, or even grammar.' He pronounced the result to be 'little short of a great failure'" (Samuel Hemphill, *A History of the Revised Version of the New Testament*, p. 96).

Dr. Cloud's book, *For Love of the Bible*, should be in the library of every Bible student. He has numerous, excellent quotes from authors from the eighteen hundreds to the present.

## Alexander Wilson McClure

Alexander W. McClure (1808-1865) reports on the 1638 revision of the AV/KJB by Dr. Samuel Ward and John Bois, two of the original Translators. He said:

In 1638, an edition revised by the command of Charles I., **for the purpose of typographical correction**, was prepared by a number of eminent scholars, among whom were Dr. Samuel Ward and Mr. Bois, two of the original

## CHAPTER 3: QUOTES FROM THE 1800s

Translators. (McClure, *The Translators Revived*, p. 222, p. 229 in the PDF)

Please note that the revision was not because of translation errors. There have been four major revisions over the years (Dr. Phil Stringer, *Ready Answers,* available on Amazon and from Dr. Stringer, Pastor of Ravenswood Baptist Church, Chicago, IL). There have been many editions of the AV/KJB over the years that contain printing errors. Therefore, the four revisions were required. McClure said:

> Among so many reprints of the Bible, and in so many different offices, it would have been a mass of miracles had not many inaccuracies crept in through error and oversight on the part of printers and correctors of the press. As this is a point on which every reader of the Bible must feel some anxiety, it may be well to make the following statement.

The statement below is from the American Bible Society, which said:

> A very able Committee of the American Bible Society, spent some three years in a diligent and laborious comparison of recent copies of the best edition of the American Bible Society, and of the four leading British editions, namely, those of London, Oxford, Cambridge, and Edinburgh, and also of the original edition of 1611. The number of variations in the text and punctuation of these six copies was found to fall but little short, of *twenty-four thousand.* A vast amount! Quite enough to frighten us, till we read the Committee's assurance, that "of all this great number, *there is not one which mars the integrity of the text, or affect any doctrine or precept of the Bible.* As this,

## THE KJB'S ACCURACY & FAITHFULNESS

however, is a point in which the minutest accuracy is to be-sought, that Committee have prepared an edition wherein these variations are set right, to serve as a standard copy, for the Society to print by in future. Infinite is the debt of gratitude which the world owes to its Maker for the Bible. Scarcely less is its debt to his goodness in raising up competent instruments for its translation into different tongues, unlocking its treasures to enrich the nations. (Andrew McClure, *The Translators Revived*, 1855, pp. 223-224, pp. 230-231 in the PDF)

Examples of supposed errors can be found throughout the literature since 1611, when the AV/KJB was first published. Almost all of the supposed errors are related to printing or publishing. Some give examples of "errors," but they are not "translational errors." For example, the "wicked" Bible that omitted "not" from Exodus 20:14:

Exodus 20:14 Thou shalt ~~not~~ commit adultery.

There are many examples like this of printing errors in the Bible, which I have placed in a work, *The History of the King James Bible*.

Similarly, the individuals who declare "translational errors" or spelling differences that affect doctrine in the AV/KJB are invariably critical of the 1611 translation. For example, James D. Price makes a considerable fuss over these aspects of different editions (Price, *King James Onlyism*, Saik Wah Press, Singapore, 2006, pp. 117-123). They cannot be claimed to be translational errors, but only that the editions differ. For a clear and easily understood explanation of these issues the student of Scripture would profit greatly by consulting

## CHAPTER 3: QUOTES FROM THE 1800s

Dr. Phil Stringer's book, *Ready Answers, A Response to the Evangelical and Fundamental Critics of the King James Bible,* available at Amazon.com

The student of Scripture must decide for himself if the differences are significant. It is the student's "soul liberty" or responsibility to interpret the text, which comes into play. In most circumstances, the resolution of the differences is easy.

What is most disconcerting is that the critics of the AV/KJB are most often associated with another translation that they consider superior. For example, Dr. Price "was the Old Testament Executive Editor and Chairman of the Executive Review Committee of the New King James Version of the Bible and a translator and section editor for the Holman Christian Standard Bible" (back cover of his book, *King James Onlyism).* This is the praxis (established practice) of most critics of the AV/KJB such as John Bellamy, previously mentioned in this work (*v.s.*).

As far as Dr. Price is concerned, he charges that Proverbs 29:18 is translated incorrectly in the AV/KJB:

> AV/KJB Proverbs 29:18: "Where there is no vision, the people perish: but he that keepeth the law, happy is he."

It is not translated incorrectly. In the New King James Version, with which Dr. Price was intimately associated, the verse is translated:

> NKJV Proverbs 29:18: Where there is no revelation, the people cast off restraint. But happy is he who keeps the law.

## THE KJB'S ACCURACY & FAITHFULNESS

His explanation for this change is an affront to every born-again believer's "soul liberty" and to be honest, denigrates the AV/KJB translators. Dr. Price says:

> Sermons built on this verse regularly interpret the word *vision* in the sense of "a sincere commitment to a worthy objective," such as "a vision for world evangelism," or "a vision for reaching the community with the gospel," or "a vision for spiritual growth and maturity." Preachers urge Christians to be "people of vision" committed to visionary goals for rescuing the perishing." (Price, *King James Onlyism*, p. 407)

He proceeds to insist that this interpretation is very wrong (see below). However, the believer has the right to interpret the passage according to his illumination by the Holy Spirit. He also has the right to accept the AV/KJB translators' **words** as accurate and faithful to the original without feeling they are less than adequate. In fact, the AV/KJB translators provided for ambiguity in Proverbs 29:18 and in many other places in the Bible for these very reasons: (1) "soul liberty" and (2) the ambiguity in the underlying "original" text. It enables the student of Scripture to draw upon his understanding and circumstances for interpretation. The student of Scripture must appropriate that the original Hebrew, Aramaic, and Greek texts contain ambiguities, which the AV/KJB translators preserved.

In Dr. Price's work, he explains and interprets the passage in Proverbs in another way, proclaiming that his interpretation is the (only) correct one. This demonstrates the way in which critics of the AV/KJB dig for any *"imagined"* error in the translation. In other words, many critics claim the translators, by the words

## CHAPTER 3: QUOTES FROM THE 1800s

they chose, caused an inappropriate interpretation in many passages. Wow! What narrow-sightedness. This should be enough evidence to mark *"with a pen of iron"* the stiffnecked, off-center, detractors of the AV/KJB and give heed to God's warning:

> *Thus saith the LORD,* **Let not the wise man glory in his wisdom**, *neither let the mighty man glory in his might, let not the rich man glory in his riches: But let him that glorieth glory in this, that he understandeth and knoweth me, that I am the LORD which exercise lovingkindness, judgment, and righteousness, in the earth: for in these things I delight, saith the LORD.*
>
> *(Jeremiah 9:23-24)*

# CONCLUSION

The AV/KJB will always be the best English version of the Bible because it is tied so wonderfully to the "original" "God-breathed" Words. And, it is translated in such a way that it will never be surpassed because of its simplicity of phrasing, beauty of words, preciseness, accuracy, faithfulness, and method and standard of translating. There are no translational errors.

John Todd said:

> [I]nstead of being *impatient* for a revision of the present text, instead of regarding what has been lately called "an improved one" with any other feeling than that of indignation against presumptuous ignorance, we shall take up THE BOOK, which from our infancy we have known and loved, with increased delight, and resolve not hastily to violate, in regard to itself, the rule which it records; "FORSAKE NOT AN OLD FRIEND, FOR THE NEW IS NOT COMPARABLE TO HIM." (Todd, 1st edition, p. 82-83) (This quote is from an apocryphal book, which this author does not believe should be included in a version of the Bible, but the truth of the sentiment is accepted. Ecclesiasticus 9:10). (my addition, HDW).

McClure said:

> "Robert Boyle, that devout son of science, on whom first the mantle of Lord Bacon fell, has said,-"I can scarce think any pains misspent that bring me in solid evidence of that great truth, that the Scripture is the word of God, which is indeed the GRAND FUNDAMENTAL" (McClure, pp. 231-232; pp. 238-239 in PDF).

> "Not that the utmost verbal perfection is claimed for the English Bible as it now stands. Some of its words have, in the lapse of time, gone out of common use; some have suffered a gradual change of meaning; and some which were in unexceptionable use two hundred years ago, are now considered as distasteful and indelicate. But the number of such words is very small, considering the' great size and age of the volume; and **the retaining of them causes but little inconvenience, compared with the disadvantages of wholesale projectors of amendment volunteered by incompetent and irresponsible schemers.**" (McClure, p. 235, p. 242 in the PDF).

In a recent article in the *Burning Bush*, Dr. Jeffery Khoo, Principal, Far Eastern Bible College said,

> Dr. Lynn Gray Gordon, a Bible-Presbyterian minister and former General Secretary of the Independent Board for Presbyterian Foreign Missions (IBPFM, in his book *The World's Greatest Truths),* rightly said, "Although the King James Version is free from error in thought, fact and doctrine, that is not to say this version is the 'inspired version.'" We agree. We reject "inspired version", "advanced revelation," and "super superiority" position of Peter Ruckman and Gail Riplinger. **Although the King James Version is not an inspired version, we nonetheless uphold it as the Word of God because it is such a faithful, accurate and reliable translation of the originally inspired and providentially preserved words of God,** and has blessed many millions of God's people throughout the 400 years of its existence. This is

no fluke, but God's approval of the work of godly and faithful translators in the time of the Reformation. So, as English readers and speakers, we are wont to stick to the good old version, the King James Version, and its good old underlying texts. (Khoo, "Seven Biblical Axioms in Ascertaining the Authentic and Authoritative Texts of the Holy Scriptures," *Burning Bush*, July, 2011, p. 78) (my emphasis, HDW)

This author could not have said it better.

## Dr. D. A. Waite's Conclusion

Recently, in an email to this author, D. A. Waite, Th.D., Ph.D., who is a well-trained Hebrew and Greek academic and who is an acknowledged scholar of the AV/KJB, said:

> "I believe that, of all the English Bible translations ever produced, the King James Bible is the most true, faithful, and accurate English translation of the verbally, plenarily, preserved original Hebrew, Aramaic, and Greek Words that underlie it."

In addition, he added the following two parts:

I. What are the "originals"?

and

II. The accuracy and faithfulness of the KJB to those "originals."

I. **The "originals:"** For the last 40 years of investigation, reading, research, speaking, and debating on this theme, I have become convinced of the following beliefs regarding the "originals":

## THE KJB'S ACCURACY & FAITHFULNESS

**(1)** I believe that the Lord Jesus Christ, and many quotations in the Bible, have clearly promised the verbal, plenary, preservation of every one of the original God-breathed Old and New Testament Hebrew, Aramaic, and Greek Words.

**(2)** I believe God has kept this promise completely.

**(3)** I believe that God has not kept His promise in Critical Hebrew texts or the Gnostic, Critical Greek texts, but rather in the Traditional Hebrew and Greek Texts.

**(4)** I believe that the specific Traditional Old and New Testament Hebrew, Aramaic, and Greek Words that God has verbally and plenarily preserved are those Hebrew, Aramaic, and Greek Words that underlie the King James Bible. In other words, these Hebrew, Aramaic, and Greek Words are the Words of the originals themselves.

**II.** **I believe that, of all the English Bible translations ever produced, the King James Bible is the most true, faithful, and accurate English translation of the verbally, plenarily, preserved original Hebrew, Aramaic, and Greek Words that underlie it.**

I base this conclusion on my careful research and documented publications on the King James Bible from Genesis through Revelation compared with three other modern translations: (1) the New King James Version, (2) the New American Standard Version, and (3) the New International Version.

In the NKJV, I document over 2,000 examples of adding, subtracting, or changing in some other way the Hebrew, Aramaic, and Greek Words.

## CHAPTER 3: QUOTES FROM THE 1800s

> In the NASV, I document over 4,000 examples of adding, subtracting, or changing in some other way the Hebrew, Aramaic, and Greek Words.
>
> In the NIV, I document over 6,650 (and I stopped counting) examples of adding, subtracting, or changing in some other way the Hebrew, Aramaic, and Greek Words.
>
> In every comparison of these three modern versions, I found the King James Bible to be the only true, faithful, and accurate translation. If I were to do the same research on any other English translation, modern or ancient, I am convinced that I would arrive at the same conclusion, that is, the King James Bible would be the most true, faithful, and accurate English translation of them all. (my emphasis, HDW)

In conclusion, the King James Bible has no translational errors. It has no mistakes. It is so accurate and faithful that, for many reasons related to time, learning, scholarship, and finances, it will never be surpassed. The voices in history echo throughout the centuries proclaiming this truth: The King James Bible **is** the Words of God in English. Let us praise God for it. Let us be thankful that we have an English Bible so well prepared under His guiding hand.

**LET US CELEBRATE THE KING JAMES BIBLE!!**

# APPENDIX

The accuracy and faithfulness of the AV/KJB is dependent upon the men who were behind the translation. This information was chosen because it is closer to the 1611 publication of the AV/KJB and because it is obvious that there was due diligence in collecting the facts; not only from the research that was done, but also from statements relating to Todd's concern for precise information. Here is John Henry Todd's account from 1818.

## THE TRANSLATORS

"If Mr. Bellamy and Sir James Burgess have allowed our Translators little knowledge that was eminently proper for their task, the world of letters has been more liberal. Their own age paid the Translators due honour, when alive; and since they were in their grave, succeeding generations have called their work blessed. As sound learning has increased, their memory indeed has risen in the estimation of the learned. And till the last period of time, we trust, the people of England "will tell of their wisdom, and the congregation will shew forth their praise." Of those among them, who have not wanted a biographer, a brief review may serve to illustrate their own as well as the character of the times. The number of them, named in the original list, as we have seen, was forty-seven; who were distributed into six classes, to meet (two of each) at Westminster, Cambridge, and Oxford.

**THE FIRST WESTMINSTER CLASS WAS COMPOSED OF THE TEN FOLLLOWING PERSONS, WHO WERE TO TRANSLATE THE "PENTATEUCH,**

AND FROM JOSHUA TO THE FIRST BOOK OF THE CHRONICLES, EXCLUSIVELY."

## 1. Lancelot Andrewes.

The celebrated Bishop of Winchester, and at that time Dean of Westminster. He was the first person named in the "(a) Order agreed upon for this Translation." It is almost sufficient to have recited only the name of this eminent person; a man always ranked among the first scholars of his time, and declared by the (b) prelate, who preached the sermon at his funeral, *to have understood fifteen languages.*

## 2. John Overal.

Dean of St. Paul's in 1604, he became afterwards Bishop of Lichfield and Coventry, and lastly of Norwich. Lord Clarendon wished that he had succeeded Bancroft in the see of Canterbury. To his learning he was solely indebted for his preferments. His (c) printed works are well known.

## 3. Adrian Saravia.

Being D.D. of Leyden, he was incorporated at Oxford; and became Prebendary of Westminster and Canterbury. He was the intimate friend of Hooker and Whitgift. He is said to have been "(d) educated in all kinds of literature in his younger days, especially in several languages."

## 4. Dr. Richard Clarke.

He had been fellow of Christ College, Cambridge; and was then (e) Vicar of Minster and Monkton, in the Isle of Thanet, and one of the Six Preachers in the

Cathedral of Canterbury. Of his learned sermons a volume in folio was published, after his death, in 1637.

## 5. Dr. Layfield.

He was fellow of Trinity College, Cambridge, and Rector of St. Clement's Danes.

## 6. Dr. Teigh.

He was Archdeacon of Middlesex, and Vicar of Allhallows Barking. This person is called by Lewis, and many others after him down to the present time, Dr. Leigh; and nothing further is mentioned. There was however, no such person Archdeacon of Middlesex. It should be Teigh or Tighe. See Le Neve's Fast. Eccl. Ang. p. 194. And also Wood, Ath. Ox. who calls this Dr. Robert Tighe "an excellent textuary, and a profound linguist; and therefore employed in the Translation of the Bible." In a (f) manuscript account of the Translators, this person is rightly called Teigh.

## 7. Mr. Burgley, or Burleigh.

Of this person, and a few more of the Translators, we know nothing further than their names. "(g) On Occasions like the present," it has been remarked, "the scantiness of biographical information is most to be lamented. All, however, that we can now glean of the characters and attainments of King James's Translators is most decidedly honourable to their memories; and from what we know of the leaders, we may fairly make an equally credible estimate of the remainder."

## 8. Mr. (h) Geoffry King.

He was fellow of King's College, Cambridge, and succeeded Mr. Spalding as (i) Regius Professor of Hebrew in that University. Our historians have hitherto mentioned no more than the name of *Mr. King*.

## 9. Mr. Thomson.

(k) He was of Clare Hall, Cambridge.

## 10. William Bedwell.

He was considered the (l) principal Arabic scholar of his time. Dr. Edward Pocock, a subsequent great master of the eastern languages, after having in his early years "(m) arrived at as a great a height in oriental learning as M. Pasor could lead him to, applied himself for further instruction to Mr. William Bedwell, Vicar of Tottenham High Cross, near London; a person, *to whom the praise of being the first, who considerably promoted the study of the Arabic language in Europe, many perhaps more justly belong, than to Thomas* Erpenius, who commonly has it. This Mr. Bedwell had made a vast progress in the knowledge of that tongue, before Erpenius had any name in the world for skill in it. And as the latter spent some time in England about the year 1606, *he was obliged to the former for many directions which he received from him in that sort of learning.* Besides several books which Mr. Bedwell published relating to it, he employed himself many years in preparing an Arabic (n) Lexicon in three volumes; and was at the pains of a voyage into Holland, to peruse the papers of Joseph Scaliger, who had made a collection, as he declared, of twenty thousand words in that language. But being, as Isaac Casaubon complained of

## CHAPTER 3: QUOTES FROM THE 1800s

him, slow in his proceeding, doubtless out of a desire that the great work he was engaged in should be as perfect as might be; at length, Golius's undertaking of the same kind, who had furnished himself to the best advantage from the East, made the publication of it useless."—Our learned Lightfoot has acknowledged the highest obligations, in his Christian and Judaical Miscellanies, for acquirements of oriental learning to Bedwell. Among Archbishop Laud's Manuscripts in the Bodleian Library at Oxford, Bedwell's commencement of a Persian Dictionary, and his Arabic Translation of the Catholic Epistles of St. John, exist. His "Arabian Trudgman," annexed to "A Discovery of the Impostures of Mahomet and of the Koran," published by him in 1615, is a very curious illustration of oriental etymology and history. It is not wonder that a man so eminent might be (o) supposed to be the same with Wlllliam Bedell, Bishop of Kilmore, (p) deeply versed in the learning also of the East. But Bishop Burnet, the biographer of Bedell, has taken no notice of this distinction; and our manuscripts and historians uniformly name Bedwell as the Translator.

**THE FIRST CAMBRIDGE CLASS CONSISTED OF THE FOLLOWING EIGHT PERSONS, TO WHOM WERE ASSIGNED "FROM THE FIRST OF CHRONICLES, WITH THE REST OF THE HISTORY, AND THE HAGIOGRAPHA, VISZ. JOB, PSALMS, PROVERBS, CANICA, ECCLESIASTES**

### 11. Edward Lively.

He was Regius Professor of Hebrew at Cambridge, and is said to have been exceeded by none of that period in acquaintance with the oriental languages.

Great was the opinion which (q) Usher, and the learned (r) Eyre, (the rest of the quote of about five words is lost, HDW)

(In 1838, Todd's 3rd edition was published. The remainder of comments concerning the translators is from his third edition. Todd made the following comments.)

He (Lively) had published in 1588 Annotations on the first five Minor Prophets, with a Latin Version of them from the Hebrew; and in 1597, the Chronology of the times of the Persian Monarchy, &c. The great oriental scholar, Pococke, has spoken of him with the highest respect. Later critics of eminence have also bowed to him as a master. He had intended a very complete Hebrew Grammar. That such a man should be appointed "one of the chiefest translators,(w)" is what of course we should expect. Being thus appointed, as Dr. Plaifere, who preached the sermon at his funeral, May 10, 1605, expresses it, his labour is minutely described by the preacher in the following words. "As soon as it was known how far in this travail he did more than any of the rest, he was very well provided for in respect of living. In his study and care, to perform well his task in the Translation, how excellently he was employed, all they can witness who were joined with him in that labour. For though they be the very flower of the University for knowledge of the tongues, yet they will not be ashamed to confess, that no one man of their company, if not by other respects, yet, at least wise for long experiences and exercise in this kind, was to be compared with him. For indeed he was so desirous that this business, begun by the commandment of our most gracious sovereign King James, should be brought

# CHAPTER 3: QUOTES FROM THE 1800s

to a happy end, that oftentimes, in many men's hearings, he protested that he had rather die, than be any way negligent herein. Which some think by all likelihood came indeed to pass: to wit, that too earnest study and pain about the Translation hastened his death. He lived blessedly: he died blessedly in the Lord. Lament, you reverend and learned University, men, that you have lost so famous a Professor, and so worthy a writer. Lament, you Translators, being now deprived of him, who no less by his merit and desert, than by the privilege of his place, was to order and oversee all your travails."

## XII. John Richardson.

Fellow of Emmanuel College, Cambridge, at that time. He became afterwards Master of Peterhouse, and then of Trinity College. One of the same name, and of the Society to which he first belonged, with whom he has been sometimes confounded, published, in 1719, "The Canon of the New Testament vindicated, in answer to the objections of John Toland;" & work of great merit, and highly commended by Leland.

## XIII. Laurence Chaderton.

He was probably the pupil of Lively. For he appears as early as in 1579, at which time Lively had been Professor of Hebrew some years, a composer of Hebrew poetry. Prefixed to the "Readings of Dr. Peter Baro upon the prophet Jonah (x)" are verses written by several Cambridge Students; among whom Chaderton is distinguished as a Greek, a Latin, and a Hebrew poet. He was renowned for his familiarity (y) with Hebrew and Rabbinical learning; and has furnished succeeding scholars with many biblical observations. At the time of undertaking the Translation he was of Christ's College, afterwards Master of Emmanuel College.

## XIV. Francis Dillingham.

He was Fellow of Christ's College, Rector of Dean in Bedfordshire (z), and author of some theological treatises.

## XV. Thomas Harrison.

Of this learned person the name and office only have been hitherto given by those, who have expressly written upon the subject of our Authorized Translation of the Holy Bible. He was Vice-Master of Trinity College, was chosen to the present task on account of his eminent (a) skill in the Hebrew and Greek languages, and for the same reason was appointed by his University a principal examiner of such as desired to excel in those tongues.

## XVI. Roger Andrewes

[He was] brother (b) of Bishop Andrewes, the first-named translator. He was Fellow of Pembroke Han; afterwards Doctor of Divinity, and Master of Jesus College. He was also a Prebendary of Chichester and of Southwell.

## XVII. Robert Spalding.

[A] scholar most accomplished in Hebrew literature, as a very learned pupil (c) and critic has recorded. He was Fellow of St. John's College, and Regius Professor of Hebrew in the University.

## XVIII Andrew Byng.

He also held the same Professorship, succeeding Mr. King in that office, whom we find in the first Westminster class of the Translator's. He was also Archdeacon (d) of Norwich. His name is misprinted *Burge* by Burnet, in his list of the Translators; and the mistake is followed by Wilkins in his Concilia (e).

**The FIRST OXFORD CLASS was composed of seven persons only, as follow; to whom were allotted the four greater Prophets, with the Lamentations, and the twelve lesser Prophets.**

## XIX. Dr. John Harding.

[T]he Regius Professor of Hebrew, and President of Magdalen College. He was also Rector (f) of Halsey in Oxfordshire.

## XX. Dr. John Rainolds, or Reinolds.

He became President of Corpus Christi College; and is the person, who, in the conference at Hampton Court, first moved the King for a new translation of the Bible. He died in May, 1607. He has been described "most prodigiously seen in all kinds of learning, most excellent in all tongues." (g) Bishop Hall relates, that "the memory, the reading, of that man, were near to a miracle (h)."

## XXI. Thomas Holland.

Of this learned person it was said, that he was "another Apollos mighty in the Scriptures (i)."

## XXII. Rickard Kilby.

He became the Rector of Lincoln College. Among the fruits of his learning, he left Commentaries on Exodus, chiefly formed from (k) the monuments of the rabbins and Hebrew interpreters. Of the care and exactness, with which our Translation was conducted, and which Dr. Kilby in his share had bestowed upon it, the following narrative by Isaac Walton, the most faithful of biographers, is a very gratifying evidence. Dr. Kilby and Bishop Sanderson had, in early life, been intimate friends. "the Doctor was to ride a journey into Derbyshire, and took Mr. Sanderson to bear him company; and they resting on a Sunday with the Doctor's friend, and going together to that parish church where they then were, found the young preacher to have no more discretion, than to waste a great part of the hour allotted for his sermon in exceptions against the late translation of several words, (not expecting such a hearer as Dr. Kilby,) and shewed three reasons why a particular word should have been otherwise translated. When Evening Prayer was ended, the preacher was invited to the Doctor's friend's house, where after some other conference the Doctor told him, he might have preached more useful doctrine, and not have filled his auditors' ears with needless exceptions against the late Translation; and for that word, for which he offered to that poor congregation three reasons why it ought to have been translated as he said, he and others had considered all of them, and found thirteen more considerable reasons why it was translated as now printed (l)!"

## CHAPTER 3: QUOTES FROM THE 1800s

## XXIII. Miles Smith.

This person was then a Canon of Hereford, afterwards Bishop of Gloucester; "which see (j)" was given him for his great pains in translating the Bible. So conversant was he, and expert, in the Chaldaic, Syriac, and Arabic, that he made them as familiar to him almost as his native tongue. Hebrew also he had at his fingers ends. For his exactness in those languages, he was thought worthy by King James to be called to that great work of the last Translation of our English Bible, wherein he was esteemed a workman that needed not be ashamed. He began with the first, and was the last man in the translation of the work; for after the task of translation was finished by the whole number set apart and designed to that business, being some few above forty, it was revised by a dozen (n) selected from them, and at length referred to the final examination of [Thomas] Bilson, Bishop of Winchester. and this our author; who, with the rest of the twelve, are styled, in the History of the Synod of Dort, "vere emimi et ab initio in toto hoc qpere versatissimi, as having happily concluded that worthy labour. All being ended, this excellent person Dr. Smith was commanded to write a Preface; which being by him done, it was made public, and is the same that is now extant in our Church Bible."

## XXIV. Dr. Richard Brett.

He was a Fellow of Lincoln College, and afterwards Rector of Quainton in Buckinghamshire. "He was a person famous in his time for learning as well as piety, skilled and versed to a criticism in the Latin, Greek, Hebrew, Chaldaic, Arabic, and Ethiopic tongues. He was a most vigilant pastor, a diligent preacher of God's

# THE KJB'S ACCURACY & FAITHFULNESS

word, a liberal benefactor to the poor, a faithful friend, and a good neighbour (o)."

## XXV. Mr. Fairclough, or Fairclowe.

[W]ho was a member of New College.

The **SECOND WESTMINSTER CLASS** contained also no more than seven, to whom the Epistles of St. Paul, and the Canonical Epistles, were consigned.

## XXVI. William Barlow.

At the commencement of the Translation he was Dean of Chester, very soon afterwards Bishop of Rochester, and lastly of Lincoln. He was one. of the learned divines selected for the conference at Hampton Court, and to him we are indebted for the valuable history of that conference, and for observations connected with it.

## XXVII. Dr. Hutchinson, or Hutckeson.

[Gustavus Paine reports his name was Ralph Hutchinson, the Westminster translator, aged about fifty-seven. He left a few notes about phrases in the New Testament. John Bois used these, which still exist in copy. They show how early the most painful re-examination of the bible text began, and how the final product came from joint efforts (Paine, *The Men Behind the KJV,* c1950s, p. 74).

## XXVIII. Dr. Spencer.

This person, we may conclude, was John Spencer, who was chosen Greek Reader in his College, (Corpus Christi, Oxford,) when only a Bachelor of Arts; who

## CHAPTER 3: QUOTES FROM THE 1800s

became afterwards a celebrated preacher, and Chaplain to the King, by whom the Translation was ordered to be made. When Dr. Rainolds, another of the Translators, died, he succeeded him as President of the College.

### XXIX. Mr. Fenton.

Probably the person who was Prebendary of Pancras in St. Paul's cathedral, afterwards D.D. and who died in 1616. See also No. XXXI.

### XXX. Mr. Rabbell.

[no information in Todd]

### XXXI. Mr. Sanderson.

One of this name, (Thomas Sanderson,) afterwards D.D. and of Balliol College, Oxford, was advanced to the Archdeaconry P of Rochester in 1606, in obedience to the King's Letter (q) which required the Bishops to seize the first opportunity of bestowing preferment on the Translators; and thus perhaps occasioned the promotion of Mr. Fenton also. See No. XXIX.

### XXXII. William Dakins.

He was Professor of Divinity in Gresham College, London; and his skill in the original languages is noticed (r) by the historian of that College.

**The SECOND OXFORD CLASS consisted of eight, to whom the four Gospels, Acts of the Apostles, and the Apocalypse, were allotted.**

### XXXIII. Thomas Ravis.

[Was] at that time Dean of Christ Church. He was afterwards Bishop of Gloucester, and lastly of London.

The means of his advancement were "eminent learning, gravity, and prudence".". His list of fellow-translators has been already noticed (t).

## XXXIV. George Abbot.

[W]ho was then (v) Dean of Winchester, and therefore Lord Clarendon is mistaken in saying (w) that he had never been a Prebendary or Dean of any cathedral. He was afterwards Archbishop of Canterbury. Wood calls him a "learned man of the old stamp." His "Exposition upon the Prophet Jonah," published in 1600, is occasionally enriched with Hebrew criticism.

## XXXV. Rickard Eedes.

He had been Dean of Worcester long before the Translation was intended, and died in November, 1604, soon after it was resolved upon, or rather begun. He was succeeded in the Deanery by Dr. James Montague; and hence, perhaps, has arisen the statement by some, that the latter and not the former person was the" Mr. Dean of Worcester" named in the original order. But Wood expressly says, that Dr. Eedes " was appointed by King James one of the number who were to translate part of the New Testaments. (x)" In another place (y) Wood omits the name of this person as of this class, and also that of Dr. Ravens, the thirty-ninth of the Translators in the King's list, mentioning those of John Aglionby and Leonard Hutten in their stead; whom we may therefore suppose to have been chosen in consequence of the death of Eedes, and of some other circumstance now forgotten respecting Ravens. I will, accordingly, after the close of the original list, give some account of these substituted persons.

## CHAPTER 3: QUOTES FROM THE 1800s

## XXXVI. Giles Tomson.

[W]ho at that time was Dean of Windsor, afterwards Bishop of Gloucester. He died in 1612, " to the great grief of all that knew the piety and learning of the man; after he had taken a great deal *of* pains, at the command *of* King James, in translating the Four Gospels, Acts of the Apostles, and Apocalypse (z)."

## XXXVII. Mr. Savile.

This was the celebrated Sir Henry Savile, of Merton College, Oxford, so well known to the learned world by his excellent edition of Chrysostom. The Lambeth Manuscript describes him as one of the Translators; and Wood, in his Annals of the University of Oxford, places him in the present list, enumerating the rest who composed it with *"chiefly Sir Henry Savile."*

## XXXVIII. John Perin.

Greek Professor at that time (a), and soon afterwards Canon of Christ Church.

## XXXIX. Dr. Ravens.

There was a person of this name of Queen's College, who in 1607 was preferred to the Sub-deanery of Wells; probably in consequence of the King's Letter. See No. XXXI.

## XL. John Harmar.

He had been Greek Professor, and was then Fellow of New College; "a most noted Latinist, Grecian, and divine (b)." He died in 1613, "having had a prime hand in the translation of the New Testament into English, at

# THE KJB'S ACCURACY & FAITHFULNESS

the command of King James, in 1604." His translation of Beza's Sermons, a book of very uncommon occurrence, bespeaks him an excellent writer of English.

**The SECOND CAMBRIDGE CLASS, consisting of seven, completes the list; and to these were consigned the *Prager of Manasses,* and *the rest of the Apocrypha.***

## XLI. John Duport, D.D.

He was Master of Jesus College, and Prebendary of Ely. Some have considered Dr. *James Duport,* who, at this time also, was Greek Professor and Fellow of Trinity College, as the person here intended.

## XLII. Dr. William Branthwait.

[W]ho at that time was of Emmanuel, afterwards Master of Gonville and Caius College.

## XLIII. Jeremiah Radcliffe.

Fellow of Trinity College.

## XLIV. Samuel Ward.

[F]irst of Emmanuel, then Master of Sidney College, and Lady Margaret's Professor of Divinity. He was the friend and constant correspondent of the profoundly learned and pious Archbishop Usher. Treasures of diversified learning, yet more especially pertaining to biblical and oriental criticism, are unfolded in their letters (c). Among this translator's *Adversaria,* in the library of Sidney College, there remain the proof of his minute attention in translating the first book of Esdras, and a collection of ancient Versions upon the beginning of Genesis.

# CHAPTER 3: QUOTES FROM THE 1800s

## XLV. Andrew Downes.

Greek Professor at that time, and sent to London from Cambridge with Bois, the translator next named, who had been his scholar·, in order to join a new selection of revisors from the whole number of the Translators, as it has been before observed (e). His remarks on Chrysostom are particularly noticed in Archbishop Usher's Letters.

## XLVI. John Bois.

[W]ho was considered one of the first Greek scholars in the kingdom, and was extremely' well acquainted with the Hebrew language, of which he had acquired the knowledge at a very early age. He was the author of a work much esteemed by the learned, for it contains a profusion of diversified and exquisite criticism gratifying the taste as well of the classical as the biblical scholar, consisting of observations' on the Four Gospels and the Acts of the Apostles. He takes occasion, in these observations, of repeatedly calling to mind *the noble work of the Translation in which he had been employed,* and of commending those who were employed with him. He wrote notes also upon Chrysostom, which Sir Henry Savile much esteemed, and used in his edition of the Works of that Father. See No. XXXIX. The valuable labours of Bois are often noticed in Archbishop Usher's Letters. To a curious work (h) upon the Greek accents, now perhaps little remembered, an elegant epistle of Bois is prefixed. In the dedication to him, by Dalechamp, of the honourable tribute to the memory of his fellow-labourer in the Translation, Thomas Harrison, (see No. XV.) he is also described as the friend of learned strangers, as well as exceeded by none in Greek learning. He died Prebendary of Ely in 1643.

## XLVII. Mr. Ward.

This person was Fellow of King's College, a Prebendary of Chichester, and Rector of Bishop's Waltham in Hampshire.

To the preceding list of the selected Greek and Hebrew scholars of a learned age and nation, which exhibits no other names as originally inserted therein, I have now to add, upon the authority of the diligent historian of Oxford and her learned writers, the names of *John Aglionby* and *Leonard Hutten.* See No. XXXV. Of the former he says, "what he hath published I find not; however, the reason why I set him down here, is, that he had a most considerable hand i*n the translation of the New Testament, appointed by King James in 1604."* Wood calls him also *an excellent linguist.* He was of Queen's College. Of the latter the historian says, after reciting his publications, "that he had a han*d in the translation of the Bible, appointed by King James,"* and speaks of him as distinguished for every kind of polite learning, and as an excellent Grecian.

## Archbishop Bancroft

There were, lastly, an overseer and an additional reviewer of the whole Translation, before the Bible of 1611 was published. The first of these, of whom the Translators speak in their Preface, and to whom they describe themselves and the whole Church of England much bound, is conjectured (i), and with good reason, to be Archbishop Bancroft. For this Prelate, Lord Clarendon asserts, "understood the Church excellently,

# CHAPTER 3: QUOTES FROM THE 1800s

and had almost rescued it out of the Calvinian party, and very much subdued the unruly spirit of the nonconformists by and after the *Conference at Hampton Court;* countenanced men of the greatest parts in learning, and disposed the clergy to a more solid course of study than they had been accustomed to; and, if he had lived, would quickly have extinguished all that fire in England, which had been kindled at Geneva (k)."

## Thomas Bilson

One of the final revisers, as already noticed (l), was Bilson, Bishop of Winchester; and of him and Dr. Miles Smith (see No. XXIII.) it has been said, "that they again reviewed the whole work; and prefixed arguments to the several books." Bilson has been considered one of the purest writers, as well as best scholars, of his time, well skilled in languages, deeply read in the Fathers and Schoolmen, and truly judicious in making use of his readings, as his excellent theological works prove.

### ENDNOTES

(a) Lewis, p. 310.
(b) (b) Buckeridge, then bishop of Rochester.
(c) Whittaker, p. 84.a—his Epitaph and Latin Speeches re among Baker's MSS. at Cambridge, vol. xxxvi. P. 417.
(d) Wood, Ath. Ox.
(e) See Lewis, p. 310, et seq.
(f) Lambeth MSS. No. 933, art, 41. Bearing the following title and date:"About the Translators, July 22, 1604."
(g) Whittaker, p. 81.
(h) Lambeth MSS. ut supra.
(i) Le Neve, Fasti Eccl. Angl. P. 412.
(j) (missing note)
(k) Lambeth MSS. ut supra.
(l) Wood, Ath. Ox. Under the article Henry Jacob. Ambrose Usher, brother of Archbishop Usher, is ranked with

## THE KJB'S ACCURACY & FAITHFULNESS

(m) Bedwell, as eminent in this kind of learning, by his contemporary Eyrem before mentioned. Parr's Collect. Of Lett. P. 11. See also Lewis's Hist. p. 339.

(m) Twells's Life of Dr. Pocock, prefixed to his Works.

(n) "the Arabic in this [Castell's] Lexicon Polyglot, will take in all, or most, of Golius, his late Arab. Lex. Printed at Leyden. For the better advancing of this work, we lent them a treasure out of our University-Library, viz. about 8 or 9 volumes MS. of Mr. Bedwell, (*who taught Erpenius,*) being a large Arabic Lexicon composed by him; the fruit of many years' labours, which he devoted to our [Cambridge] Library." Dr. Worthington Lett. To Hartlib, (1661,) p. 282.

(o) See Mr. Whittaker's Hist. and Crit. Enq. p. 81- 85

(p) Bedell accompanied Sir Henry Wotton to Venice in 1604, where the most considerable addition, which he made to his learning "was in the improvement of the Hebrew," and in the acquirement of "rabbinical learning." Bp. Burnet's Live, &c. of Bp. Bedell, p. 20 See also p. 260.

(q) See Parr's Collect. Of letters to and from Archbishop Usher, pp. 3, 4.

*(r)* William Eyre, or Eyres, was of Emmauel College, Cambridge. We find him, in 1607, detailing to Archbishop Usher his previous labour upon a critical illustration of the Sccriptures; therein maintaining the *verity of the original text*, and summing up his many valuable biblical remarks into this consclusion: *Sola Hebraici Veteris Instrmenti edition, sicut Graeca Novi, authentica est it pura..* See Parr's Collect. ut supr. pp. 5, 11. Dr. Ward, one of the Translators of our Version, has described him "eminent in the Hebrew tongue." Ibid. p. 26. There are other letters from Eyre to Usher, in the collection, whence the preceding information has been taken; of which the most curious is that upon the subject of *the Hebrew punctuation*. See also what he says of Lively, ibid. p. 3.

*(s)*
*(t)*
*(u)*
*(v)*

## CHAPTER 3: QUOTES FROM THE 1800s

(w)  (From this point on, the endnotes switch to the third edition of Todd's work. There are more footnotes in the first part of Todd's third edition than the first edition, so they begin at (w) for this part of his work.) Sermon at his funeral, Dr. Plaifere's Sermons, 8v0. 1616, p. 202, seq.

(x)  Published in 1579. This work is in Latin, abounding with important Hebrew criticisms.

(y)  These his attainments, and others also, are detailed in the biography of him by Dr. William Dillingham, Cantab. 1700.

(z)  Lambeth MSS. ut supra.

(a)  Recorded in an oration by C. Dalechamp, at Cambridge, 1632, p. 7.

(b)  Lambeth MSS. ut supra.

(c)  Thomas Gataker, the eminent biblical scholar, in his treatise on the New Testament, Lond. 1648, p. 7.

(d)  Lambeth MSS. ut supra.

(e)  Vol. iv. p. 432.

(f)  Lambeth MSS. ut supra.

(g)  In Wood's Athenae Oxon.

(h)  Decad. Of Epistles, 1608, p. 74.

(i)  Wood, Ath. Oxon.

(j)  (note missing in Todd's work.)

(k)  Wood, Ath. Oxon.

(l)  Walton, Life of Bishop Sanderson.

(m)  Wood, Ath. Oxon.

(n)  The writer of a Life of Mr. Bois tells us, that .the whole work being finished, and three copies of the whole Bible sent to London, viz. one from Cambridge, a second from Oxford, and a third from Westminster; a new choice was to be made of two out of each company, *six in all,* to review the whole work and polish it, and extract one out of all the three copies, to be committed to the press. For the dispatch of this business, Mr. Andrew Downes and Mr. John Bois were sent for up to London out of the Cambridge

# THE KJB'S ACCURACY & FAITHFULNESS

company; where meeting their *four fellow-labourers,,* they went daily to Stationers-Hall, and in three quarters of a year fulfilled their final task." Lewis, Hist. Transl. p. 323. But "the English divines at Dort, in 1618, giving an account of this affair to the Synod, say they were *twelve*. This agrees with the number of the companies, which were six, two in each of the three places. And Dr. Samuel Ward, one of the English divines delegated to that Synod, was himself concerned in the Translation, and therefore must know that circumstance." Ward's lives of the Prof. of Gresham Coll. p. 47.

(o) Wood, Ath. Oxon
(p) Le Neve, Fasti Eccl. Ang.
(q) See the letter at the close of this compilation.
(r) Ward, Lives of the Gresham Professors, p. 46.
(s) A Wood, Ath. Oxon.
(t) See before, p. 14, note K. (This note reads: "The copy of the King's instructions, which Bishop Burnet received from Dr. *Ravis, one of the Translators,* and has printed in his Hist. of the Reformation, some writers, in their account of this Translation, have overpassed. *The fifteenth* instruction *complete* is found only in this copy. I will notice any material variations.")
(u) This note is missing
(v) Le Neve, ut supra.
(w) Hist. of the Rebellion, *b. i.*
(x) Ath. Oxon.
(y) Annals of the Univ. of Oxford, *b. i.*
(z) Wood's Ath. Oxon.

(a) Le Neve, Fasti Eccl. Ang.
(b) Wood's Ath. Oxon.
(c) Parr's Collect. of the Archbishop's Letters, &c. 1686, passim. There is an encomaistic (high praise) poem, of some merit, upon Dr. Ward, in John Hall's Poems, Cambridge, 1646, p. 48. In one of Archbishop Ushers letters to this learned person, there is a note of an error in

# CHAPTER 3: QUOTES FROM THE 1800s

the Preface of our Translators to the Bible, in 1611, viz. of *Efnard*; which the Archbishop observes should be Einard; or rather Eginhard; Eginhardus, according to Olearius. It was no doubt, at firt, merely an error of the press, but it has continued, and is found even in the learned Dr. Blayney's edition of the Bible.

(d)  So the learned Abraham Wheelock informs Archbishop Usher. Parr's Collect. p. 329.
(e)  See before, p. 36 *note* n.
(f)  Biograph. Brit. and Dr. Whittaker, p. 88.
(g)  Entitled, "Veteris Interpretis cum Beza aliisque recentioribus Collatio in Quatuor Evangeliis et Apostolorum Actis, &c."
(h)  Tractatus de Tonis in Lingua Graec. R. Franklin, S. T. B. Lond. 1633.
(i)  By Archbiship Newcome, Hist. View, &c. p. 104.
(j)  Missing note
(k)  Hist. of the Rebellion, b. i.
(l)  See before, p. 37.

# INDEX

Abbot, 102
accuracy, 10, 13, 16, 17, 18, 20, 46, 49, 52, 55, 58, 63, 64, 69, 78, 83, 85, 89
Aglionby, 102, 106
Alexander Geddes, 52
American Bible Society, 65, 77
Andrewes, 90, 96
Arabian Trudgman, 93
Arabic, 26, 46, 67, 69, 92, 99, 108
Augustine, 26
Balliol, 101
Bancroft, 24, 37, 90, 106
Bedell, 93, 108
Bedwell, 92, 108
Bellamy, 26, 30, 31, 32, 33, 34, 35, 36, 79, 89
Bilson, 99, 107
Bodleian, 93
Bois, 14, 15, 76, 100, 105, 109
Branthwait, 104
Brett, 99
Bristol, 54
Broughton, 36, 37, 38, 39, 47
Brown, 12
Burgess, 34, 35, 36, 89
Burgley, 91
Burgon, 37, 38, 63, 65, 66, 67, 117
Burnett, 24, 25
Byng, 97
Calcutta, 61
Cambridge, 14, 19, 26, 34, 35, 36, 38, 58, 77, 89, 90, 91, 92, 93, 95, 105, 107, 108, 109, 110
Cappellus, 47
Castell, 46, 108
Cattermole, 41, 43
Chaderton, 95
Chaldee, 46
Chaplin, 22
Christ College, 36, 38, 90
Chrysostom, 14, 103, 105
Clarendon, 90, 102, 106
Clarke, 57, 58, 61, 62, 63, 70, 90
Conference, 37, 41, 63, 107
contemporary, 23, 32, 34, 36, 53, 108
Corpus Christi College, 14, 97
Cox, 57
Cruttwell, 29, 33, 34
Dakins, 101
Dean of Canterbury, 8, 67

Dedication, 49
degree of conformity, 16, 18
degree of refinement, 16
Deism, 33
Derbyshire, 21, 98
Dillingham, 96, 109
Downes, 14, 15, 105, 109
Duport, 104
Eedes, 102
Emmanuel College, 95, 96
ENDLESS DIVISION, 70
English versions, 25, 29, 68
Erpenius, 92, 108
Ethiopic, 46, 69, 75, 99
Eyre, 94, 108
Fairclough, 100
Fairclowe, 100
Fenton, 37, 101
Field, 41
fifteen rules, 24
fifty-four, 24, 32
foundation, 17, 18, 26, 35
Geneva, 24, 29, 46, 107
Geoffry King, 92
Gloucester, 41, 99, 101, 103
Gomez, 44
good Christian Reader, 25
Grecian, 103, 106
Greek, 8, 12, 13, 14, 17, 18, 20, 22, 24, 25, 26, 38, 45, 46, 49, 53, 58, 60, 61, 64, 65, 66, 67, 74, 75, 76, 80, 85, 86, 87, 95, 96, 99, 100, 103, 104, 105, 106, 118, 119, 120
Gresham, 101, 110
Gustavus Paine's, 49
Hales, 32
Hampton Court, 37, 41, 97, 100, 107
Harding, 97
Harmar, 103
Harrison, 96, 105
Hebraist, 36, 39, 47, 54
Hebrew, 12, 13, 17, 18, 20, 21, 22, 24, 25, 26, 30, 31, 33, 34, 35, 36, 38, 39, 45, 46, 47, 48, 49, 52, 53, 57, 67, 69, 70, 80, 85, 86, 87, 92, 93, 94, 95, 96, 97, 98, 99, 102, 105, 106, 108, 109, 118, 119, 120
Holland, 92, 97
Hutchinson, 100
Hutckeson, 100
Hutten, 102, 106
imperfect, 33
inerrant, 17
infallible, 17
Jacobin, 58
Khoo, 84, 85
Kilbie, 21
Kilby, 13, 21, 98

## ABOUT THE AUTHOR

King James, 2, 3, 9, 11, 12, 13, 14, 15, 18, 24, 37, 40, 41, 46, 47, 49, 58, 62, 63, 67, 69, 71, 78, 79, 80, 84, 85, 86, 87, 91, 94, 99, 102, 103, 104, 106, 117, 119, 120
Koran, 93
Lady Margaret's Professor, 104
Lambeth Manuscript, 103
Lancelot, 90
Latin, 24, 30, 31, 46, 53, 70, 94, 95, 99, 107, 109, 121
Latin Vulgate, 30, 31, 121
Latinist, 103
Layfield, 91
Lewis, 44, 45, 91, 107, 108, 110
Lightfoot, 46, 93
Lively, 93, 94, 95, 108
Lowth, 55
LXX, 9, 30, 31
Mahomet, 93
Malan, 8, 67, 72, 73, 74, 75, 76
Master of Peterhouse, 95
McClure, 4, 40, 43, 49, 76, 77, 78, 83, 84
Merton, 103
Middleton, 61, 72
Miles Smith, 99, 107
Minor Prophets, 94
Montague, 102
Moorman, 17
Nicholson, 18
Norton, 58
oriental, 46, 92, 93, 94, 104
Overal, 90
Oxford, 14, 19, 47, 51, 55, 77, 89, 90, 93, 100, 101, 103, 106, 109, 110
Paine, 100
Paragraph Bible, 58
Paraphrase, 118
paraphrastic, 69
Pasor, 92
Perin, 103
Persian, 46, 93, 94
Plaifere, 94, 109
Pococke, 46, 47, 94
Polyglot, 46, 61, 108
Poole, 44, 45
precise, 16, 17, 18, 27, 89
precision, 12, 17, 18, 52
Preface, 25, 99, 106, 111
Prelate, 106
Principal, 84
Purpose, 19, 25
Quarterly Review, 10, 27, 34, 35, 36, 57, 58
Rabbell, 101
Rabbinical, 95
Radcliffe, 104
Rainolds, 36, 37, 41, 97, 101

Ravens, 102, 103
Ravis, 24, 101, 110
rector, 21
Regius, 92, 93, 96, 97
Reinolds, 97
Rennell, 58, 60
Revisionists, 64, 65, 66
Richardson, 95
Riland, 57
Riplinger, 44, 84
Robert Gray, 54
Rodriquez, 44
Ruckman, 84
rules, 24, 53
RVG, 44
Samaritan, 46
Samuel Horsley, 53, 54
Sanderson, 21, 98, 101, 109
Saravia, 90
Savile, 14, 15, 103, 105
Scribner, 49
Selden, 14, 15, 46
Septuagint, 9, 30, 31, 36, 69, 117
slide rule, 16
Smith, 37, 99
Socinianism, 33, 34, 59, 60
Spanish, 44, 46
Spencer, 100
Stringer, 11, 77, 79
Swift, 51
Syriac, 46, 69, 75, 99
Teigh, 91
testimony of history, 26
textual basis, 32

The Key, 54, 55
Thomson, 92
Todd, 10, 22, 23, 24, 25, 27, 29, 30, 31, 32, 33, 34, 36, 38, 39, 43, 46, 47, 50, 52, 53, 55, 58, 61, 83, 89, 94, 101, 109
Toland, 95
Tomson, 103
Trinity College, 91, 95, 96, 104
Tyndale, 29, 45
Ussher, 46
Vance, 37, 49
Vicar, 90, 91, 92
Vulgate, 30, 31, 36, 69
Waite, 64, 67, 85, 119
Ward, 14, 76, 104, 106, 108, 110
Wegner, 38
Westminster, 14, 19, 89, 90, 97, 100, 109
Whittaker, 26, 28, 34, 35, 71, 107, 108, 111
Wood, 91, 102, 103, 106, 107, 109, 110
Worcester, 102

# ABOUT THE AUTHOR

Dr. Williams was born in Ft. Pierce, Florida, July 11, 1941. He was saved at the age of fourteen at his local Baptist church under Pastor J. R. White where he was active in the church youth group. His local church ordained him to preach the gospel. After graduating with honors from high school, he attended Stetson University where he met his wife, Patricia, and they were married in 1961. Starting in the ministerial program at Stetson and switching to pre-med in his junior year, he graduated with honors with a B.A. After Stetson, he taught high school at Eau Gallie, Florida for two years, and then continued his training at the University of Miami Medical School where he graduated with honors and induction in AOA medical honorary in his junior year. Following his medical training, Dr. Williams and Patricia settled in New Port Richey, Florida where he practiced Family Medicine as a board certified family practitioner. He was active in his community as a hospital board member for twenty years, a chief-of-staff, president of the medical society, an advisory board member and president of Moody Bible Institute's Florida program, a board member of the Health Planning Commission, and a teacher at his local Baptist church. He helped develop and administrate a multi-specialist medical clinic with forty thousand patients and seventeen doctors. His Biblical training was obtained at Stetson University, Moody Bible Institute, and Louisiana Baptist University. After retirement, Dr. Williams has continued serving the Lord Jesus Christ as an associate pastor, a teacher, as vice-president and representative for the Dean Burgon Society (recently resigned), and member of the King James Bible Research Council. He received a Ph.D. in Biblical studies at Louisiana Baptist University. He has traveled to many foreign lands where he has represented the Dean Burgon Society, has taught courses to pastors and has participated in evangelistic events. He is author of the several books, *The Lie That Changed The Modern World; The Miracle of Biblical Inspiration; Word-For-Word Translating of the Received Texts, Verbal Plenary Translating; Hearing the Voice of God; The Septuagint is a*

*Paraphrase; The Pure Words of God; The Attack on the Canon of Scripture; Origin of the Critical Text; Wycliffe Controversies;* and *The Covenant of Salt* in addition to many articles and booklets. Some of his articles can be reviewed at this web address:

http://www.theoldpathspublications.com/TOPArticles.html.

Dr. Williams and his wife, Patricia have two sons, five grandchildren, and five great-grandchildren. They recently celebrated their 50th wedding anniversary. He and his wife are the directors of The Old Paths Publications, which specializes in print-on-demand (POD) and ebooks. The purpose of their endeavor is to help authors of Biblically sound books make their works available to the public by reducing the upfront costs of printing, storing, and shipping books, by printing the books in the US, England (EU), and Australia, and by listing books on Amazon worldwide.

(October, 2011)

## BOOKS BY DR. WILLIAMS

(Available on Amazon)

## THE MIRACLE OF BIBLICAL INSPIRATION

This 130-page book is a refutation of perfection of translations (Idealism), derivative inspiration, double inspiration, thought or message inspiration, partial inspiration, natural inspiration, neo-orthodox inspiration, and inspiration of men. The book explains the true Words of God were "given by inspiration of God" and "once delivered" to the apostles and prophets in Hebrew, Aramaic, and Greek. The process and product is a one-time miracle!

## ABOUT THE AUTHOR

## WORD-FOR-WORD TRANSLATING OF THE RECEIVED TEXT, VERBAL PLENARY TRANSLATING:

Pastor D. A. Waite said: This 270 page perfect bound book may be purchased through www.BibleForToday.org or Amazon.com. The book is a polemic for proper translating. There is a vital need for a book to inform sincere Bible-believing Christians about the proper techniques of translating the WORDS of God into the receptor languages of the world. No book like this one has ever been written. It is a unique and much-needed book. The very first requirement for any translation of the Bible is to have the proper WORDS of Hebrew, Aramaic, and Greek from which to translate. It is the contention of this book that the original verbally and plenarily inspired Hebrew, Aramaic, and Greek WORDS have been verbally and plenarily preserved in accordance with God's promises. These preserved WORDS are those received-text-WORDS which underlie the King James Bible. This volume emphasizes the requirement of a proper technique to be used in all translations of God's WORDS. It must be done in a verbally and plenarily translation technique. That is, the Hebrew, Aramaic, and Greek WORDS must be conveyed into the receptor languages, not merely the ideas, concepts, thoughts, or message. This technique is absent in all of the other manuals on Bible translation. Dr. Williams is not the usual sort of writer. He combines the meticulous skill of a Doctor of Medicine with the artistry and acumen of a Doctor of Philosophy to produce this grand volume. May translators and sincere Christians of all persuasions and professions use this important book worldwide! Amazon.com (type in book title) or The Bible For Today Press, BFT #3302 ISBN 1-56848-056-3, Order by PHONE: 1-800-JOHN 10:9, Order by FAX: 856-854-2464, Order by MAIL: Bible For Today, 900 Park Avenue, Collingswood, NJ 08108"

## THE ATTACK ON THE CANON OF

## SCRIPTURE, A POLEMIC AGAINST MODERN SCHOLARSHIP

This 172 page perfect bound book was released in January, 2008. ISBN 978-0-9801689-0-7. This book demonstrates the newest attack on the Words and books of the Bible by modern day scholarship. The changing methods for assaulting the Scriptures are important for those who are concerned about the relentless attempt to destroy them. In a remarkable polemic against modern scholarship, Dr. Williams outlines the most recent means many are using to undermine confidence in the Words of God received through the priesthood of believers. It will be available at Amazon.com. (type in book title) or at BibleForToday.org, BFT # 3345.

## THE LIE THAT CHANGED THE MODERN WORLD

This book is in perfect bound format, 440 pages in all. ISBN 1-56848-042-3. It is a factual defense not only of the King James Bible, but also of the Hebrew and Greek Words that underlie the King James Bible. The author is a medical doctor, now retired, who has researched this important topic thoroughly. May the Lord Jesus Christ use and honor this study in the days, weeks, months, and years ahead until our Lord Jesus Christ returns. It should be in every layman's library, every Pastor's library, every church library, every college library, every university library, and in every theological seminary library. It is available through Amazon.com (type in book title) or Bible For Today Press, www.biblefortoday.org, BFT # 3125.

## THE PURE WORDS OF GOD

This is a perfect bound 136 page book. ISBN 978-0-9801689-1-4. Dr. Williams' book, *The Pure Words of God,* clarifies the use of the word "pure" when it is used to define the Words of God. Should "pure" be applied to translations, to Traditional/Received Texts, or to critical texts? Once the correct application is explained, Dr. Williams clarifies God's commands to receive and keep His pure Words. It is available

# ABOUT THE AUTHOR

through Amazon.com (type in the book title) or Bible For Today Press at www.biblefortoday.org, BFT #3344.

## WYCLIFFE CONTROVERSIES

This 311 page perfect bound book is about Dr. John de Wycliffe (1324?-1384). He is an important person in the history of the Bible and Bible Translating. This book is an attempt to recognize and place in one book the contradictions and confusion surrounding the Wycliffe and his colleagues. For example, are the Wycliffe Bible Versions based upon Old Latin Texts close to the received Text or are the closer to Alexandrian Texts that influenced Jerome's Latin Vulgate? In addition, many other questions have been raised in the literature such as who were Wycliffe's close associates who participated in the work; where and when did the Lollards that were associated with him originate; and many other controversies. Dr. Williams provides some evidence for most likely answers to a number of questions. It is a perfect bound, 311 pages. It is available through Amazon.com (type in book title) or Bible For Today Press at www.biblefortoday.org, BFT #3363.

## HEARING THE VOICE OF GOD

This 311 page perfect bound book discusses the critical factors related to the postmodern confusion surrounding this issue. The subject is clearly and realistically approached from a plenary Biblical approach. Mysticism accompanying this issue is refuted. This work investigates the topic as it relates to revelation, conscience, inspiration, illumination, and the voice of the Lord in Scripture. Dr. Williams explains how postmodern philosophy has created an atmosphere that contributes to the confusion surrounding this issue. It is available through Amazon.com (type in book title) or Bible For Today Press at www.biblefortoday.org, BFT #3340.

## ORIGIN OF THE CRITICAL TEXT

# THE KJB'S ACCURACY & FAITHFULNESS

This 157 perfect bound book examines the origin of the text that underlies the modern versions called 'Bibles.' There are five significant pivotal points pertain to the origin of corrupted Critical Texts that lie behind the modern versions of the Bible. It is important for believers to understand the origin and the influence of these original language texts on doctrine, practice, application, and translation of these false texts. At least one new English version of the Bible has appeared in the marketplace every six months for the last several decades that is translated from these false texts.

## THE COVENANT OF SALT

This 118-page book is an examination of the use of "salt" in Scripture and in literature over the centuries. The word "salt" and the "covenant of salt" are frequently misunderstood. Dr. Williams investigates the use of the word in Scripture and draws some amazing and relevant conclusions concerning this intriguing word.

CPSIA information can be obtained
at www.ICGtesting.com
Printed in the USA
JSHW031810171222
35006JS00003B/113